Maths

10 Minute Tests

8-9 years

Test 1: Shape and Space

Test time: 0 — 5 — 10 minutes

1

Which 3D shape does this net show?

_____

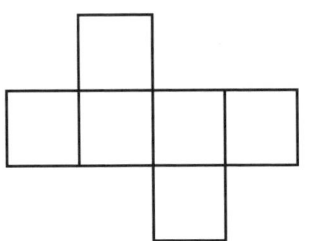

2

Circle the horizontal line.

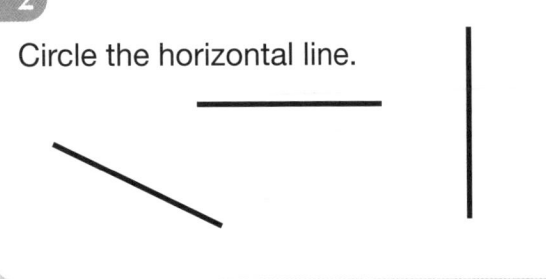

3

Find the area of this shape that is made up of 1 cm squares.

_____

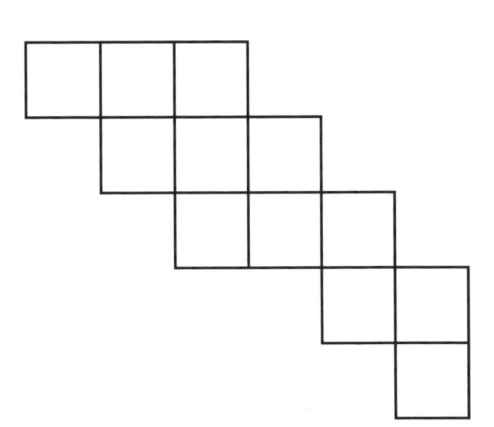

4

Sanjeev's school day starts at 8:55 in the morning.

Draw this time on the clock face.

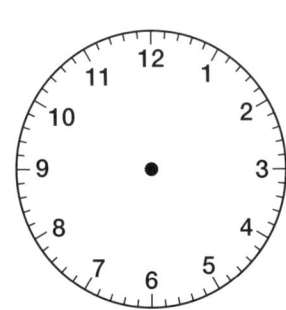

5

How many degrees are there in a whole turn?

Circle the correct answer.

A 180°   B 90°

C 360°   D 100°

6

Draw a pentagon.

7

Hannah is making jelly.

This jug shows how much water she needed for the recipe.

How much water did Hannah need?

_____ ml

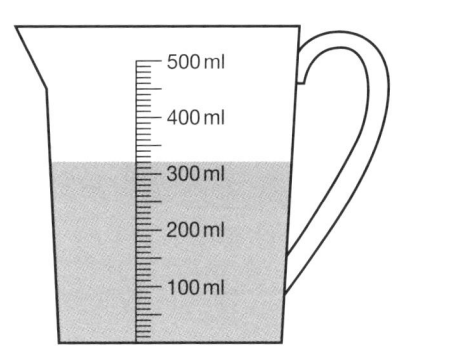

8

What is the name of this 3D shape?

_____

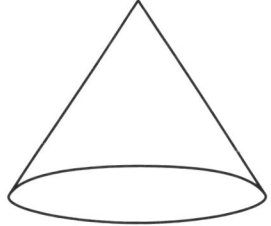

9

These children want to walk to the pond. Circle the direction in which they need to walk.

A SW   **B** NW   **C** SE   **D** NE

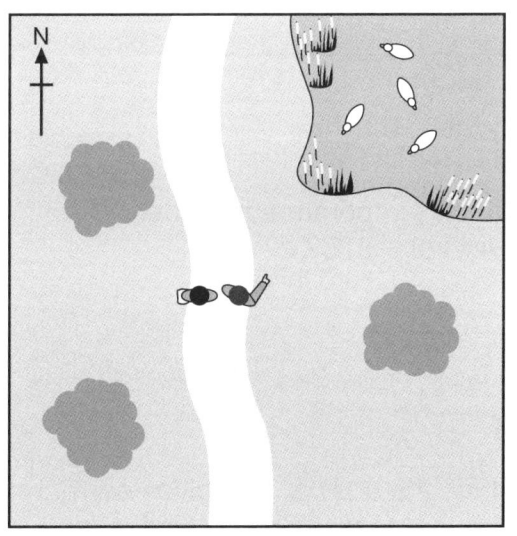

10

Find the perimeter of this rectangle.

_____ cm

8 cm

2 cm

Test 2: Number

Test time: 0 — 5 — 10 minutes

1 Find double 45.

_____

2 What fraction would need to be added to $\frac{6}{10}$ to make 1?

_____

3 Put these numbers in order, smallest first.

5555   555   5050   505

____ ____ ____ ____

4 Which temperature is higher, −4°C or −8°C?

_____

5 Circle the answer that gives correct answers to all these multiplication facts.

5 × 3   7 × 7   6 × 4   9 × 6

A 15, 48, 24, 54   **B** 15, 48, 26, 54

C 16, 49, 24, 45   **D** 15, 49, 24, 54

6 Find the remainder.

69 ÷ 8 = 8 r_____

7 Write the missing number in this sequence.

47   31   ____   −1

8 Add the correct symbol: <, > or =

24 + 39 ____ 9 × 8

9 Freya has £23.89.
How many pence in total does she have?

_____ p

10 Add together 40, 70 and 60.

_____

Test 3: Shape and Space

Test time: 0 — 5 — 10 minutes

1 How many grams equal 1 kilogram?

_____ g

2 In what units are angles measured?

_____

3 How many lines of symmetry does this shape have?

_____

4 What is the area of a square that is 4 cm by 4 cm?

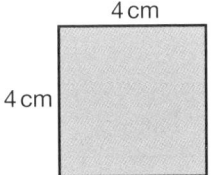

_____ cm²

5 Complete this sentence.

There are _____ weeks in one year.

6 Is this a regular or irregular polygon?

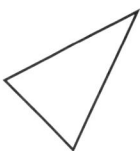

_____

7 What time is this clock showing?

_____

8 How many right angles are there in one whole turn?

_____

9 Which unit of measure would you use to find the mass of a bag of sweets?

_____

10 Circle the angle that is greater than 45°.

A B C D

Total

TEST 4: Data Handling

1-2

Class 4 – Favourite colour survey	
Colours	Tally
Red	
Yellow	||||
Pink	
Blue	|||| ||
Green	|||
Purple	|||| |
Brown	||

This tally chart shows Class 4's favourite colours.

Pink is liked the same as blue. Red is liked half as much as purple.

Use this information to complete the tally chart correctly.

What is the least favourite colour? _____

3-5

Look carefully at the pictogram.

Who read the least number of books during the summer holidays?

_____

How many books did Meena read?

_____

How many books were read altogether?

_____

Number of books read during the summer holidays.

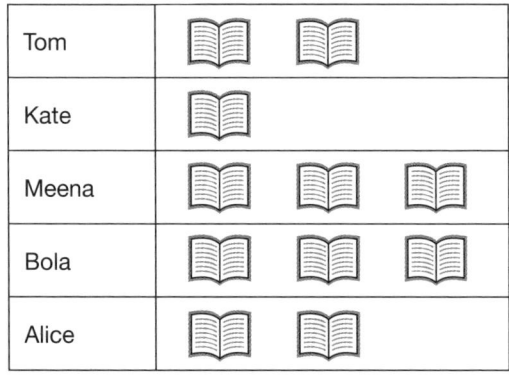

= 2 books

6-7

Place these numbers correctly in the Venn diagram.

6 18 21 19 7 15 12

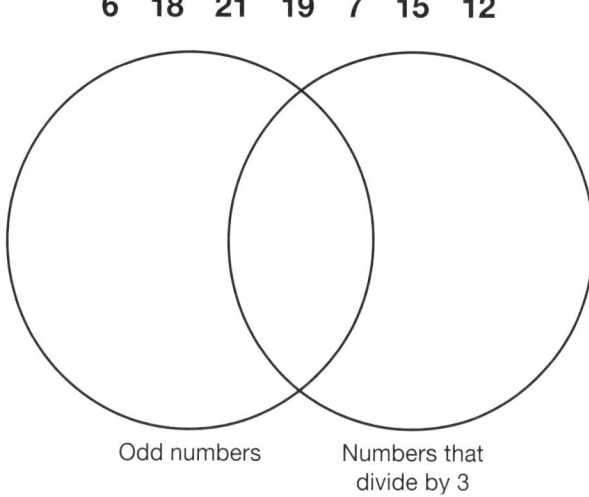

Odd numbers   Numbers that divide by 3

8-10

Look carefully at this bar chart.

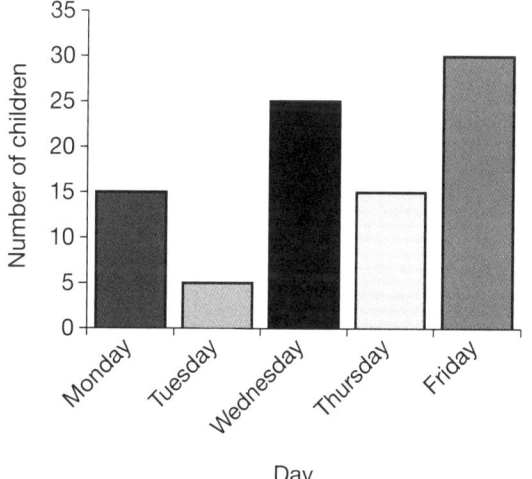

Number of children walking to school during the first week in October

How many children walked to school on Wednesday?

_____

Which day of the week do you think had the best weather?

_____

Why do you think the least number of children walked to school on Tuesday?

_____

_____

TEST 5: **Number**

Test time: 0 5 10 minutes

1

What is the digit 2 worth in this number?

7209

Circle the answer.

A two units **B** two tens

C two hundreds **D** two thousands

2

Circle the number that equals 9×9.

49 56 81 78 109 63

3

Subtract 9 from 7821.

____

4

Izzy was given 33 colouring pencils. She shared them equally with two friends.

How many pencils did they each get?

______

5

$\frac{1}{8} + \frac{6}{8} =$ ______

6

With an arrow, mark −3 on this number line.

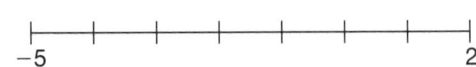

7

Continue the number sequence.

85 77 69 61 ____ ____

8

Which of the following weights is heavier?

3.4 kg or **4.3 kg**

____

9

Circle the factor pair for 63.

6 and 3 9 and 7 10 and 6

10

Round 24.3 to the nearest ten.

____

Total

Test 6: Shape and Space

Test time: 0 – 10 minutes

1 Which unit would you use to measure how long it takes you to brush your teeth in the morning?

_____

2 Name this shape.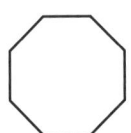

_____

3 Before Dan left for school, he looked at the clock.

It takes him 15 minutes to walk to school. What time will he arrive?

_____

4-5 Look at the grid below.

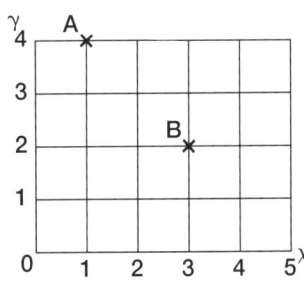

Point A is found at: 1 square along and 4 squares up. This is written as (1, 4).

Point B is at (____, ____)

Mark point C on the grid at (5, 3).

6 How many faces does a cuboid have?

_____

7 Circle the capital letter with no lines of symmetry.

T   A   J   W

8 How many sides does a heptagon have?

_____

9-10 Draw two different rectangles with a perimeter of 14 cm.

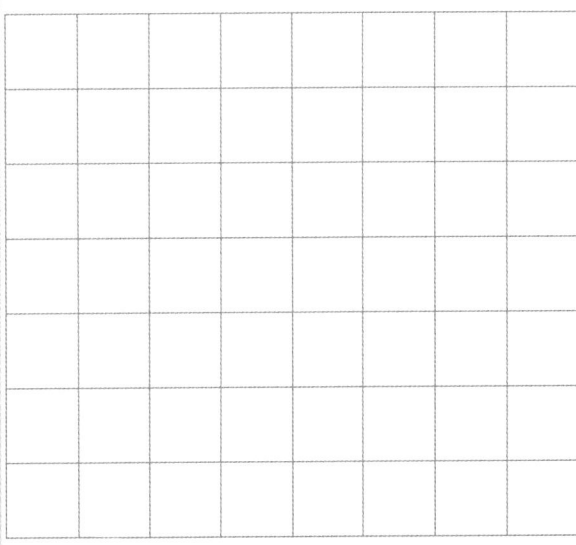

Time for a break! Go to Puzzle Page 38

TEST 7: Data Handling

Test time: 0 — 5 — 10 minutes

1-2

Look at this bar chart carefully.

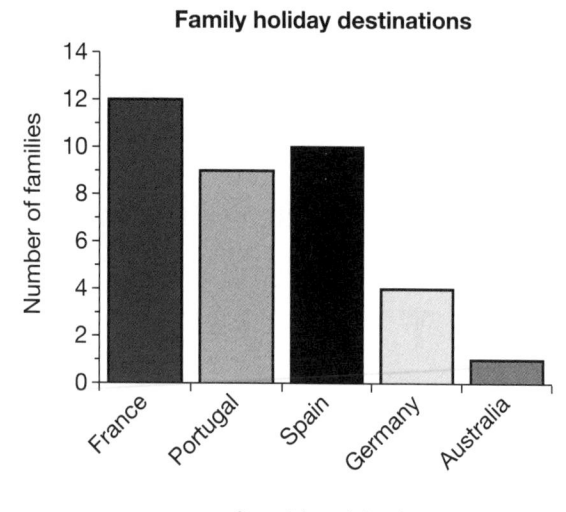

Family holiday destinations

Which country is visited by the most families?

_____

Why do you think only one family visited Australia?

_____

_____

_____

_____

3-5

Put this information into the pictogram below.

Day	Monday	Tuesday	Wednesday	Thursday	Friday
cm of rain	1	3	1	5	3

Pictogram showing the rainfall for a week in April.

Monday					
Tuesday					
Wednesday					
Thursday					
Friday					

💧 1 cm of rain

On which day did the most rain fall? _____

What was the total amount of rainfall for the days shown? _____ cm

6-7

Add these numbers to the Carroll diagram.

      5   12   20

Why are there no numbers in the empty section of the diagram?

_____

_____

_____

	Odd	Even
Numbers in the 5 × table	25, 15	10
Numbers in the 6 × table		18, 24

8-10

Put the information from the table into the bar chart.

Favourite ice cream	Vanilla	Chocolate	Strawberry	Mint	Raspberry
Number of children	6	8	10	3	4

Survey showing which ice cream the children in Class 4T liked the best.

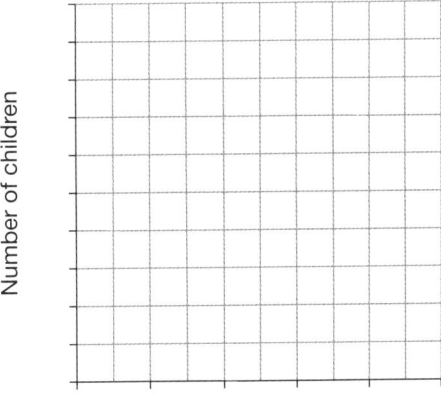

Ice cream flavour

How many children are there in Class 4T? _____

Test 8: Number

1 Complete this roman numeral sentence.

_____ − VII = XV

2 Put these numbers in order, smallest first.

2.3   2.1   3.2   1.2   2.2

____ ____ ____ ____ ____

3 Halve 86.

____

4 Circle the two numbers which would complete this number sentence.

56 = _____ × _____

A 6, 7   B 7, 7   C 8, 8   D 7, 8

5 Write a decimal fraction between 1.5 and 1.8.

____

6 Write the number nine thousand, seven hundred and three.

____

7 Write the fraction of the shape that is shaded.

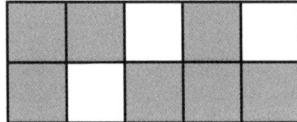

____

8 Is 25 a multiple of 5?

____

9 There were three Year 4 classes in Budleigh School. Each class had 28 children.

How many children were there in Year 4?

____

10 Will the answer of this number sentence be an odd or even number?

23 + 79   ____

TEST 9: Shape and Space

1

Complete this shape.

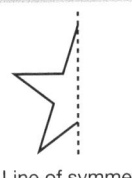

Line of symmetry

2-3

Complete this bus timetable.

Malmesbury	8:30	9:00	
Crudwell	8:40		9:40
Oaksey	8:50	9:20	9:50

4

Draw a line of symmetry on this shape.

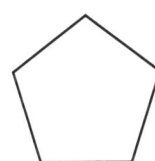

5

How many years are there in a millennium?

_____

6

The Hooper family squeezed apples from their apple tree to make homemade apple juice. After 20 minutes they had squeezed 650 ml.

How many more millilitres would make a litre of apple juice?

_____ ml

7

What is the perimeter of a 5 cm × 8 cm rectangle?

_____ cm

8

Order these angles, largest first. Circle the correct answer.

A 1, 2, 3   **B** 2, 3, 1

C 3, 1, 2   **D** 3, 2, 1

9

Draw a quadrilateral.

10

Complete this sentence.

2670 g is the same as _____ kilograms and _____ grams.

Test 10: Number

1

12 kg of raspberries were picked. They were split equally between 4 families.

How many kilograms of raspberries did each family get?

_____

2

Write a number that is a multiple of both 4, 5 and 10.

_____

3

Write the temperature shown on this thermometer.

_____

4

Round 1679 to the nearest hundred.

_____

5

Circle the decimal that is equivalent to $\frac{4}{10}$.

A 0.4   **B** 4.0   **C** 0.04   **D** 0.44

6

Find the answer.

$23 \times 6 =$ _____

7-8

Add the fourth number in this sequence.

1st	2nd	3rd	4th	5th
22	34	46	___	70

In which position will the first number be over 100?

_____

9

Circle the sign that should replace the •.

$98 • 32 = 66$

A +   **B** −   **C** ×   **D** ÷

10

Order these fractions, largest first.

$\frac{1}{2}$ $\frac{8}{10}$ $\frac{3}{5}$

_____ _____ _____

Test 11: **Problem Solving**

Test time: 0 — 5 — 10 minutes

1

Class 4's PE lesson finished at 11:45. It lasted for 50 minutes.

What time did the PE lesson start?

_____

2

Aimee spent half of her savings on a DVD.

How much did she have originally if the DVD cost £12.50?

£ _____

3-4

Leon and Kyle collect 6 spiders. A spider has 8 legs.

How many legs in total do the 6 spiders have? _____

The next day they collect 6 more spiders.

How many legs in total do all the spiders have now? _____

5

Explain how you would find the perimeter of a 5 cm by 15 cm rectangle.

_____

_____

_____

6

In the number sentence below find the missing digit.

△△ + △8 = 50

Each △ = the same digit.

△ = _____

7

Donna has thought of a number. She adds 5 to it, then multiplies it by 5. The answer is 50.

What number did Donna start with? _____

8-9

On a visit to the fair Finn bought 3 toffee apples.

Each toffee apple cost £1.49.

How much did the toffee apples cost in total?   £ _____

How much change was Finn given when he handed over £10.00 to pay for them?   £ _____

10

What is the missing operation?

70 ✶ 4 = 280

✶ = _____

TEST 12: Data Handling

Test time: 0 – 5 – 10 minutes

1-2

Pictogram showing the number of brothers and sisters of children in Year 4

Number of brothers and/or sisters	Number of children
0	☺ ☺
1	☺ ☺ ☺ ☺
2	☺ ☺ ☾
3	☺ ☾
4	☾

 = 10 children

Look carefully at the pictogram and answer the questions.

How many children have three brothers and/or sisters? _____

How many children are there in Year 4? _____

3-5

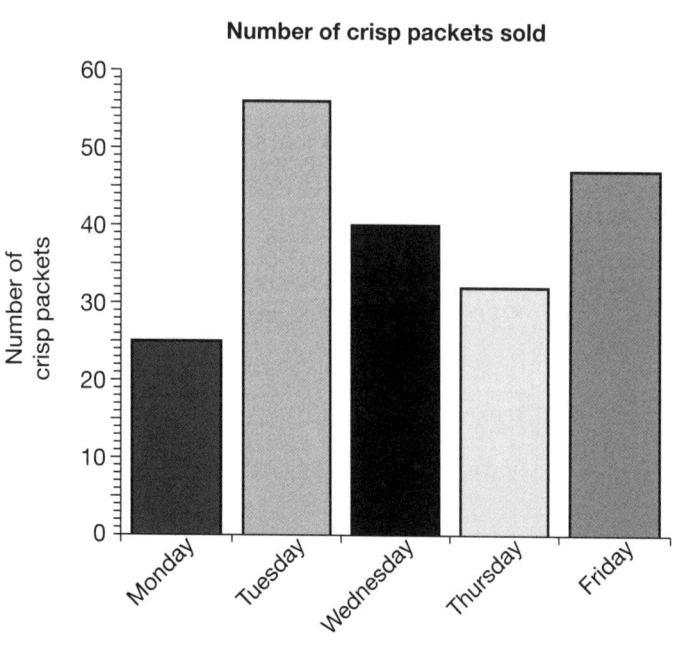

Describe what information this bar chart shows.

_____
_____
_____
_____

On which day are the fewest packets of crisps sold?

_____

How many more crisps were sold on Tuesday than on Thursday?

_____

6-10

Complete this frequency table then draw a bar chart to represent the data.

Survey showing how children in Class 4B like their potatoes cooked.		
Potato type	Tally	Total
Mash		7
Roast	|||| ||||	
Chips		9
Jacket		5

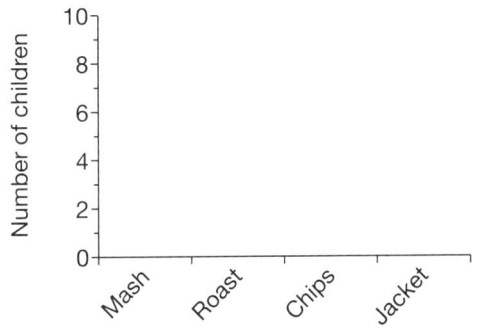

Class 4B's favourite way to eat potatoes

Look carefully at the information above and answer the questions.

How many children are in Class 4B? _____

30 children from Class 4T completed the survey, and the results were added to Class 4B's tally. Half of Class 4T liked chips, none of the class liked mash and 10 children liked roast potatoes.

What is the new total for chips? _____

What is the new total for jacket potatoes? _____

Time for a break! Go to Puzzle Page 39

Test 13: Number

Test time: 0 – 5 – 10 minutes

1 Write the number 7107 in words.

_____

_____

_____

2 What is $\frac{1}{2}$ of £18.00?

£ _____

3 How many sevenths are needed to make 1?

_____

4 Write these numbers in descending order.

24.4   20.8   24.8   20.4

_____ _____ _____ _____

5 Add the missing number.

2900 ÷ _____ = 290

6 Add any two numbers to this number sentence so that it reads correctly.

_____ > _____

7 Round £67.49 to the nearest pound.

£ _____

8 Add the missing number.

_____ + 450 = 1000

9 Double 39.

_____

10 Write the rule for this sequence.

98   83   68   53   38

_____

_____

_____

Total

Test 14: **Problem Solving**

Test time: 0 – 5 – 10 minutes

1

Which pair of numbers has a sum of 14 and a product of 49?
Circle the correct answer.

A 6, 7   **B** 7, 7   **C** 6, 8   **D** 7, 8

2

Niall rode his bike from 3:38 p.m. to 7:00 p.m. when he was called in for tea. How long had Niall been riding on his bike?

_____ hrs _____ mins

3

Tim thinks of a number. He multiplies it by 9 and the answer is 63.
What was his original number?

_____

4

In this calculation the same digit is missing from two places. Circle the value for the missing digit.

☐7 − 3☐ = 58

A 9   **B** 8   **C** 7   **D** 6

5

Write a number story for: **16 × 4 = 64**

_____
_____
_____
_____

6-7

Katie bought a 3 kg bag of carrots to feed her guinea pigs. It took the guinea pigs 5 days to eat 1 kg.

How many days did the 3 kg of carrots last? _____

How many kilograms of carrots will the guinea pigs eat in the month of November? _____ kg

8

What three consecutive numbers total 33?

_____ _____ _____

9-10

A packet of sweets cost 45p.

How many packets of sweets can be bought for £5.00? _____

How much change would be left? _____

TEST 15: **Mixed**

Test time: 0 5 10 minutes

1

How many lines of symmetry does this shape have?

_____

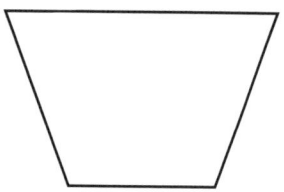

2

Jess's chickens laid 5 eggs a day for 28 days.

How many eggs did they lay in total? _____

3

Complete this Venn diagram using the numbers provided.

10   16   6   20   24   18

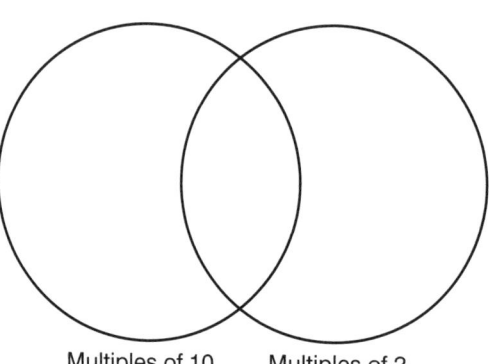

Multiples of 10   Multiples of 2

4

Total 80, 40, and 90.

_____

5

Round £47.75 to the nearest pound.

£ _____

6

On Crudwell Primary School's sports day 98 children needed to be split into 7 groups. How many children were in each group?

_____

7

Find the area of this shape that is made up of 1 cm squares.

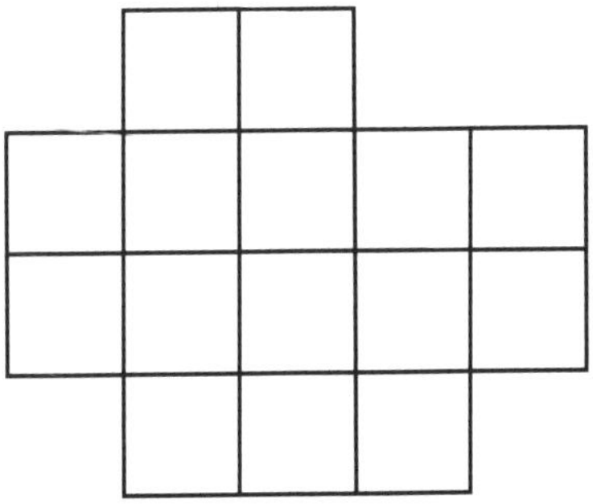

_____

8

Which angle is larger than a right angle?
Circle the correct answer.

A 46°   **B** 90°   **C** 105°   **D** 79°

9

What fraction of this shape has been shaded?

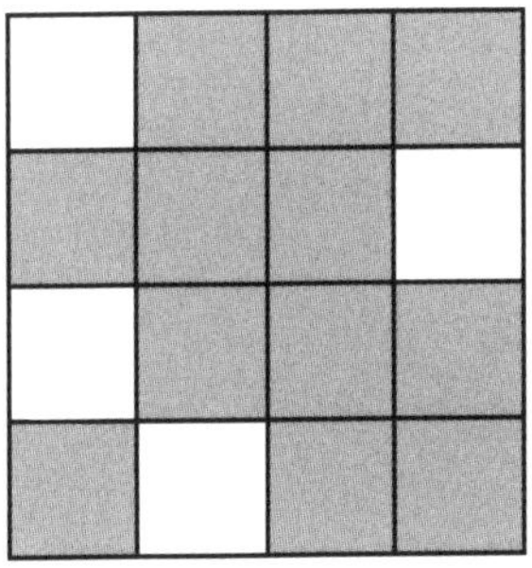

_____

10

Name a 3D shape with two flat faces and one curved face.   _____

TEST 16: **Mixed**

Test time: 0 — 5 — 10 minutes

1-2

Show 12:27 p.m. on this clock face.

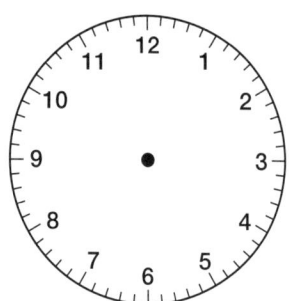

What will the time be in 1 hour and 13 minutes time?

_____

3

Circle the correct answer.
2003 to the nearest 10 is

A 2010   B 2030   C 2000   D 1990

4

Complete this number sequence.

79   66   53   ____   27   ____

5

Which two angles equal one whole turn?

A 100° and 250°   B 90° and 270°
C 110° and 260°   D 170° and 180°

6-7

Look carefully at this table.

Child's name	Number of blackberries picked
Lisa	20
Hannah	30
Kyle	44
Dan	12
Jodie	27
Tyler	8

Who picked the most blackberries?

_____

Did the girls or the boys pick more blackberries?

_____

8

Halve 42.   _____

9

A bottle holds 1000 ml of juice. Unfortunately it was knocked over and 450 ml of juice was spilt.
How much juice is left in the bottle now?

_____

10

Divide 8 by 10.   _____

Total

Test 1: Shape and Space (pages 2–3)

1. **cube** A net, when cut out and folded along the lines shown, will form a 3D shape.
2. ▬▬▬▬▬▬▬
   A horizontal line goes from left to right, a vertical line goes up and down and a sloping line is diagonal.
3. **12 cm²** Count the squares to find the area.
4. Moving around a clock face, each number represents 5 minutes. Use the numbers on the clock to count up in 5s: the minute hand points to 11 to show 55 mins. The hour hand is shown just before the 9 as it moves from 8 to 9.

5. **C**
6. Any 5-sided shape is a pentagon, e.g.

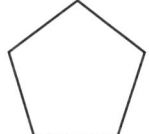

7. **320 ml** Between each 100 ml, the jug has been separated into 10 equal parts. Therefore each small line represents 10 ml (100 ml ÷ 10 = 10 ml). The grey shaded area is shown level with 320 ml.
8. **a cone** A cone has a circular face and a curved face that narrows to a point.
9. **D** Moving clockwise around a compass, the directions are: North, East, South, West. The pond is halfway between north and east from the children, therefore it is north-east.
10. **20 cm** To find the perimeter of a shape, add the measurement of each side. The opposite sides of a rectangle will be the same length or width; 8 + 8 + 2 + 2 = 20

Test 2: Number (page 4)

1. **90** Use column multiplication, making sure to work from right to left and add on any numbers carried over.

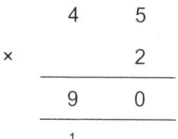

2. $\frac{4}{10}$ When adding fractions, only the top numbers (numerators) are added and the bottom numbers (denominators) remain the same; 1 is the same as $\frac{10}{10}$ so the equation is $\frac{6}{10} + \square = \frac{10}{10}$; $\frac{6}{10} + \frac{4}{10} = \frac{10}{10}$

3. **505, 555, 5050, 5555** Put the numbers in a place value grid, as shown. The numbers with the fewest digits will be the smallest, so begin with these. Look for the smallest number in the first column (hundreds): if any numbers are the same, find the smallest number in the next column. Repeat with the four-digit numbers, starting in the thousands.

Th	H	T	O
5	5	5	5
	5	5	5
5	0	5	0
	5	0	5

4. **−4°C** Negative numbers 'mirror' whole numbers, as shown on this number line: the numbers increase in size from left to right.

   −8 −7 −6 −5 −4 −3 −2 −1 0 1 2 3 4 5 6 7 8

5. **D** 5 × 3 = 15; 7 × 7 = 49; 6 × 4 = 24; 9 × 6 = 54
6. **5** Invert the sum from division to multiplication and use knowledge of times tables to help: 8 × 8 = 64 so subtract 64 from 69 to find a remainder of 5.
7. **15** To find missing numbers in a sequence, calculate the difference between two numbers next to one another:
   47 − 31 = 16 so 16 is subtracted each time.
   31 − 16 = 15; 15 − 16 = −1
8. **<** '<' means less than and '>' means greater than; 24 + 39 = 63; 9 × 8 = 72; 63 < 72
9. **2389p** £1 = 100p so multiply by 100. Place the number in a decimal grid and, because 100 has 2 zeros, move the number 2 places to the left to find the answer.

Th	H	T	O		t	h
		2	3	•	8	9
2	3	8	9	•		

10. **170** 4 + 7 + 6 = 17 so 40 + 70 + 60 = 170

Test 3: Shape and Space (page 5)

1. **1000 g**
2. **degrees (°)**
3. **3** Lines of symmetry go through the middle of the shape, creating a 'mirror image' on each side of the line.

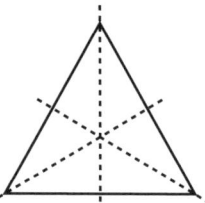

4. **16 cm²** To find the area of a square, multiply the lengths of 2 sides: $4 \times 4 = 16$
5. **52**
6. **irregular** All sides are the same length on a regular polygon and are different lengths on an irregular polygon. Only 2 sides are the same length so it is irregular.
7. **33 minutes past 11 or 27 minutes to 12 or 11:33** A clock face is separated into 5 minutes between each number, so use the numbers on the clock to count up in 5s. The minute hand has just moved past 6 (5 mins × 6 = 30 mins) and is pointing to 3 minutes after (30 + 3 = 33). The hour hand is shown halfway between 11 and 12 as the hour moves towards 12.
8. **4** A right angle is 90° and a whole turn is 360°; 90 + 90 + 90 + 90 = 360
9. **grams** Mass means the weight of an object, so the answer will be kilograms or grams. Grams are the most appropriate measurement here.
10. **B** Option A is about 45° as it is half the size of a right angle and options C and D are even smaller. Therefore only B can be the right answer.

Test 4: Data Handling (pages 6–7)

1–2. **Red = |||,**
Pink = |||| ||
Brown is the least favourite colour. 7 children liked blue, so 7 also liked pink; 6 children liked purple, so 3 liked red (6 ÷ 2 = 3); only 2 children liked brown.

3–5. **Kate, Meena read 6 books, 22 books were read in total.** Each book icon represents 2 books; Kate read 2 books; 3 × 2 = 6 books read by Meena; 11 × 2 = 22 books read altogether.

6–7. As 21 and 15 are odd numbers and can be divided by 3, they are placed in the section where the circles overlap. As 19 and 7 are odd numbers that cannot be divided by 3, they are placed in the remainder of the left circle. As 12, 6 and 18 can be divided by 3 and are not odd numbers, they are placed in the remainder of the right circle.

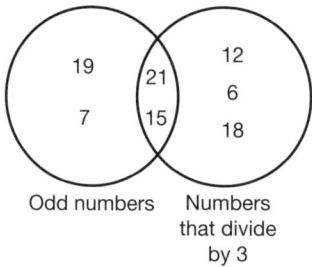

Odd numbers   Numbers that divide by 3

8–10. **25 children, Friday, e.g.** *Only 5 children walked to school on Tuesday because the weather was very wet.* To read a bar chart, look at the number that the top of each bar is level with (it helps to place a ruler at the top of the bar to find the number). The black bar representing Wednesday is level with 25; Friday is most likely to have had the best weather as this is the day most children walked to school.

Test 5: Number (page 8)

1. **C** Refer to Test 2 Q3 and use the place value grid to help find the answer. Write the number in the grid; 2 is in the hundreds place therefore it is **two hundreds**.
2. **81**
3. **7812** Round 9 to 10 and subtract (7821 − 10 = 7811); because 9 was rounded, 1 too many has been subtracted so add this back on (7811 + 1 = 7812).
4. **11 pencils each** There are 3 children including Izzy, so the equation is 33 ÷ 3 = □; invert the equation from division to multiplication and use times tables knowledge to find the answer: 3 × 11 = 33
5. $\frac{7}{8}$ Refer to Test 2 Q2 on adding fractions.
6.

Refer to Test 2 Q4 on negative numbers.
7. **53, 45** Refer to Test 2 Q7 on sequences; 8 is subtracted each time: 61 − 8 = 53; 53 − 8 = 45
8. **4.3 kg** The weight with the larger whole number will be heavier.
9. **9 and 7** Factor pairs are 2 numbers that are multiplied together to make another number: 9 × 7 = 63
10. **20** When rounding a number to the nearest 10, look at the number in the ones column. If it is 4 or below, leave the number in the tens column

unchanged. If it is 5 or above, raise the number in the tens column by one. Then put a zero in the ones column. Here, the 2 remains in the tens column and the number rounds down to 20.

Test 6: Shape and Space (page 9)

1. **minutes**
2. **octagon** Any 8-sided shape is an octagon.
3. **8:40 a.m., 08:40 or 20 to 9** On a digital clock, the first 2 digits show the hour and the second 2 digits show the minutes; 25 mins + 15 mins = 40 mins
4–5. **(3, 2)** When writing coordinates, always write however many squares along it is first.

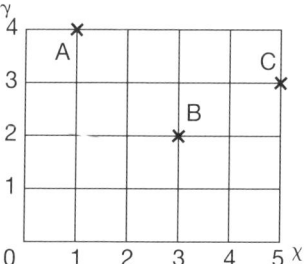

6. **6 faces** A face is a flat side of a solid object. A cuboid is a shape with faces that are rectangles or squares, for example, a cereal box.
7. **J** Refer to Test 3 Q3 on symmetry.
8. **7 sides**
9–10. **2 of the following possible answers: a 4 by 3 rectangle, a 5 by 2 rectangle, a 1 by 6 rectangle.** Refer to Test 1 Q10 on perimeter. Half of 14 = 7 so 2 sides of the rectangle must add up to 7 cm. For example, 4 + 3 = 7 and 4 + 4 + 3 + 3 = 14

Test 7: Data Handling (pages 10–11)

1–2. **France, e.g.** *because it's far away and expensive to fly to.* Refer to Test 4 Q8–10 on reading bar charts.

3–5.

Monday	💧				
Tuesday	💧	💧	💧		
Wednesday	💧				
Thursday	💧	💧	💧	💧	💧
Friday	💧	💧	💧		

Thursday, 13 cm of rain 5 cm is the highest measurement; 1 + 3 + 1 + 5 + 3 = 13

6–7.

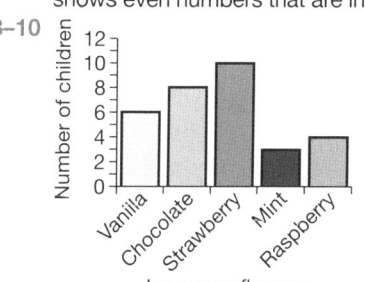

There aren't any odd numbers in the 6 times table. The top left square shows odd numbers that are in the 5 times table; the top right square shows even numbers that are in the 5 times table; the bottom left square shows odd numbers that are in the 6 times table; the bottom right square shows even numbers that are in the 6 times table.

8–10.

31 children There are 5 different flavours, so the bottom of the chart needs to be divided into 5 equal sections and 0 to 10 needs to be inserted on the left-hand side (this can be in 2s, as shown). Each flavour is represented by a 'bar' that is level with the number shown in the table; 6 + 8 + 10 + 3 + 4 = 31

Test 8: Number (page 12)

1. **XXII** VII = 7 and XV = 15, so the equation is ☐ − 7 = 15; invert the equation by changing it to addition (7 + 15 = 22); 22 = XXII
2. **1.2, 2.1, 2.2, 2.3, 3.2** Insert the numbers into a place value grid ensuring the decimal points are lined up. Look for the smallest number in the first column; if any numbers are the same, find the smallest number in the next column.

2	.	3
2	.	1
3	.	2
1	.	2
2	.	2

3. **43** Partition the number by breaking it down into tens and ones (86 = 80 + 6) and divide both numbers by 2 (80 ÷ 2 = 40 and 6 ÷ 2 = 3). Finally, add the answers together, 40 + 3 = 43
4. **D** Use knowledge of times table to help: 7 × 8 = 56

5 **1.6 or 1.7** A decimal fraction is the same as a decimal number; the digits after a decimal point increase in the same way as whole numbers (1.5, 1.6, 1.7, 1.8).
6 **9703** Refer to Test 2 Q3 and write the number in a place value grid to help find the answer.
7 **$\frac{7}{10}$** There are 10 squares altogether, so this is the denominator (bottom number); 7 are shaded so this is the numerator (top number).
8 **yes** A multiple is the answer when numbers are multiplied together, therefore multiples of 5 are the answers in the 5 times table: $5 \times 5 = 25$
9 **84** Refer to Test 2 Q1 on column multiplication; $28 \times 3 = 84$
10 **even** The last digit in each number is odd and when 2 odd numbers are added together they will always make an even number: $3 + 9 = 12$ and $23 + 79 = 102$

Test 9: Shape and Space (page 13)

1 Refer to Test 3 Q3 on symmetry.

2–3 Find the difference between times shown next to one another. Moving down the table, the difference between 8:30 and 8:40 is 10 mins, so add this to 9:00 to find the time for Crudwell (9:10). Looking at the Oaksey row, the difference between 9:20 and 9:50 is 30 mins, so add this to 9:00 to find the third time for Malmesbury (9:30).

Malmesbury	8:30	9:00	**9:30**
Crudwell	8:40	**9:10**	9:40
Oaksey	8:50	9:20	9:50

4 **e.g.**

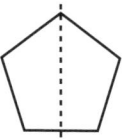

Refer to Test 3 Q3 on symmetry.
5 **1000**
6 **350 ml** 1 litre = 1000 ml; use column subtraction, making sure to borrow from the top number in the next column if the number being subtracted from is smaller. When borrowing from zero, always change it into a 9 and borrow from the next column instead.

7 **26 cm** Refer to Test 1 Q10 on perimeter; $5 + 5 + 8 + 8 = 26$
8 **C** The further apart the ends of the lines are, the larger the angle.
9 **any closed 2D shape made of four straight lines** A quadrilateral is a shape with 4 sides.
10 **2670 g is the same as 2 kilograms and 670 grams** 1000 g = 1 kg so 2000 g = 2 kg; 2670 g − 2000 g = 670 g

Test 10: Number (page 14)

1 **3 kg** $12 \text{ kg} \div 4 = 3 \text{ kg}$
2 **e.g. 20, 40** Refer to Test 8 Q8 on multiples; $4 \times 5 = 20$ and $2 \times 10 = 20$
3 **−7°C** Refer to Test 2 Q4 on negative numbers. Between each 10°, the thermometer has been separated into 10 equal parts. Therefore each small line represents 1° (10° ÷ 10 = 1°). The grey shaded area is shown level with −7°C.
4 **1700** When rounding a number to the nearest 100, look at the number in the tens column. If it is 4 or below, leave the number in the hundreds column unchanged. If it is 5 or above, raise the number in the hundreds column by one. Then put a zero in the tens and ones columns. Here, 6 is in the hundreds place and the number to its right is 7, so 6 increases by 1 and the numbers after it become 0.
5 **A** $\frac{4}{10}$ = 4 tenths. Refer to the place value grid in Test 2 Q9 and insert 4 into the tenths place; there is no digit before the decimal point so a zero is placed before it.
6 **138** Refer to Test 2 Q1 on column multiplication.
7–8 **58, 8th position (106)** Refer to Test 2 Q7 on sequences; 12 is added each time and $46 + 12 = 58$; continue adding 12 (70 + 12 = 82; 82 + 12 = 94; 94 + 12 = 106)
9 **B** Because the answer is less than 98, the equation will be division or subtraction; $98 \div 32 = 3$ remainder 2 and $98 − 32 = 66$
10 **$\frac{8}{10}, \frac{3}{5}, \frac{1}{2}$** Draw a table with one row separated into tenths, one row into fifths and one row in half. Shade in the fractions on the table to see the difference in size.

$\frac{1}{2}$					$\frac{1}{2}$				
$\frac{1}{10}$	$\frac{1}{10}$	$\frac{1}{10}$	$\frac{1}{10}$	$\frac{1}{10}$	$\frac{1}{10}$	$\frac{1}{10}$	$\frac{1}{10}$	$\frac{1}{10}$	$\frac{1}{10}$
$\frac{1}{5}$		$\frac{1}{5}$		$\frac{1}{5}$		$\frac{1}{5}$		$\frac{1}{5}$	

Test 11: Problem Solving (page 15)

1. **10:55 or 5 to 11** Count back to 11:00 by subtracting 45 mins; 50 − 45 = 5 mins left to subtract; 5 mins before 11 is 10:55.
2. **£25.00** Partition the amount into pounds and pence (£12.50 = £12.00 + 50p) then multiply the numbers by 2 (£12 × 2 = £24.00 and 50p × 2 = £1.00). Finally, add the answers together £24.00 + £1.00 = £25.00

3–4. **48, 96** 6 × 8 = 48; 6 + 6 = 12 spiders; 12 × 8 = 96

5. **Child's own words, e.g.** *The perimeter of the rectangle is found by adding together 2 × 5 cm and 2 × 15 cm or 5 cm + 5 cm + 15 cm + 15 cm* Refer to Test 1 Q10 on perimeter.
6. **2** 8 is shown in the ones place in one of the numbers and when 8 subtracted from any number in the 10s, the answer will always have 2 in the ones place; therefore the second triangle will be 2, as will the others: 22 + 28 = 50
7. **5** Write the equation as a missing number sentence: □ + 5 × 5 = 50. Work backwards through the equation, completing the inverse (divide instead of multiplying, subtract instead of adding, etc.): 50 ÷ 5 = 10 and 10 − 5 = 5

8–9. **£4.47, £5.53** Use column addition, making sure to add any numbers that are carried over. Line up the decimal points and always work from right to left, in the same way as adding a number without a decimal.

```
      1 . 4 9
      1 . 4 9
  +   1 . 4 9
  ─────────────
      4 . 4 7
        1 2
```

To find the amount of change, one way is to convert the amount to pence to make the calculation easier and refer to Test 9 Q6 on column subtraction; £1.00 = 100p so £10.00 = 1000p and £4.47 = 447p ; 1000 − 447 = 553; 553p = £5.53

10. **✗** Because the answer is larger than both numbers, the equation must be addition or multiplication; 70 + 4 = 74 and 70 × 4 = 280

Test 12: Data Handling (pages 16–17)

1–2. **15 children, 105 children** 1 smiley face = 10 children so $\frac{1}{2}$ a smiley face = 5 children; 10 + 5 = 15; 9 whole smiley faces = 90 (9 × 10 = 90) and 3 halves of a smiley face = 15 (3 × 5 = 15); 90 + 15 = 105

3–5. *It shows the number of packets of crisps sold between Monday and Friday.*, **Monday, 24** Refer to Test 4 Q8–10 on reading bar charts and use the title and labels to help. Between every 10 packets, the chart has been separated into 10 equal parts, so each small line represents 1 packet (10 ÷ 10 = 1); Monday = 25; Tuesday = 56 and Thursday = 32; 56 − 32 = 24

6–10.

Survey showing how children in Class 4B like their potatoes cooked.		
Potato type	Tally	Total
Mash	||||| ||	7
Roast	||||| ||||	9
Chips	||||| ||||	9
Jacket	|||||	5

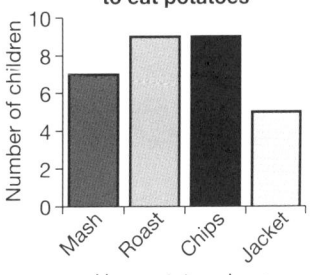

Class 4B's favourite way to eat potatoes

30 children, chips = 24, jackets = 10 Refer to Test 4 Q8–10 on bar charts. 7 + 9 + 9 + 5 = 30 in Class 4B. 15 liked chips in 4T (30 ÷ 2); 9 + 15 = 24 liked chips in total. Add the amounts given for 4T (15 chips + 0 mash + 10 roast = 25) then subtract the answer from 30 children to find how many like jacket potatoes (30 − 25 = 5). Finally, add the amounts for 4B and 4T (5 + 5 = 10 liked jacket potatoes in total).

Test 13: Number (page 18)

1. **Seven thousand, one hundred and seven** Refer to Test 2 Q3 – writing the number in the place value grid can help find the answer.
2. **£9.00** 18 ÷ 2 = 9 so £18.00 ÷ 2 = £9.00
3. **7** $\frac{7}{7}$ is the same as 1 whole.
4. **24.8, 24.4, 20.8, 20.4** Refer to Test 8 Q2 on ordering decimals.
5. **10** Refer to the place value grid in Test 2 Q9; 2900 has been moved one place to the right, therefore it has been divided by 10
6. **Any numbers where the first number is larger than the second, e.g. *234 > 125*** > means 'more than'.

7 **£67.00** Refer to Test 5 Q10 and Test 10 Q4 on rounding; here, 7 is in the pounds place and 4 is to its right, so 7 remains the same and the following digits change to 0.
8 **150** Invert the sum to 1000 − 850 and refer to Test 9 Q6 on column subtraction.
9 **78** Refer to Test 2 Q1 on column multiplication; 39 × 2 = 78
10 **Rule = −15** Refer to Test 2 Q7 on sequences; 98 − 83 = 15

Test 14: Problem Solving (page 19)

1 **B** Add the numbers to find the sum and multiply numbers to find the product: 7 + 7 = 14 and 7 × 7 = 49
2 **3 hrs 22 mins** Use a number line to calculate the elapsed time, as shown.

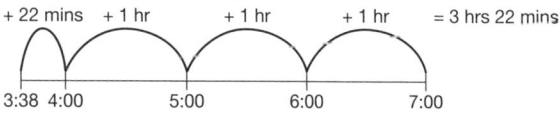

3 **7** The equation is □ × 9 = 63; use times table knowledge or invert the equation to a division (63 ÷ 9 = 7).
4 **A** In the options shown, only 9 can be subtracted from a number that has 7 in the ones place to give an answer that has 8 in the ones place; **9**7 − **3**9 = 58
5 **Child's own number story for 16 × 4 = 64**, e.g. *4 children each collected 16 conkers. In total the four children collected 64 conkers.*
6–7 **15 days, 6 kg** 1 kg = 5 days so multiply by 3 (3 × 5 = 15); there are 30 days in November and 30 ÷ 5 days = 6 kg
8 **10, 11, 12** As 3 consecutive numbers need to be found, divide 33 by 3 (33 ÷ 3 = 11); this number is in the middle, then subtract 1 and add 1 to find the numbers either side: 10 + 11 + 12 = 33
9–10 **11 packets, 5p** £5.00 = 500p; multiply by 10 to find an answer nearer 500 (45 × 10 = 450) and continue adding 45 (450 + 45 = 495); 10 lots of 45 + 1 lot of 45 = 11; 500 − 495 = 5

Test 15: Mixed (pages 20–21)

1 **1** Refer to Test 3 Q3 on symmetry.

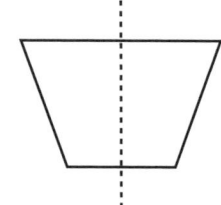

2 **140 eggs** Refer to Test 2 Q1 on column multiplication; 28 × 5 = 140
3
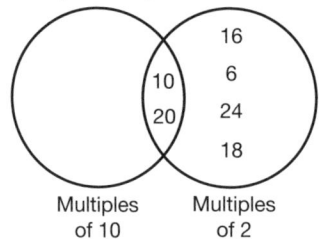

Refer to Test 8 Q8 on multiples. Both 10 and 20 are multiples of 10 and 2 so they are placed in the section where the circles overlap. There are no other multiples of 10, so the rest of the left circle remains empty. Because 16, 6, 24 and 18 are all multiples of 2 but not multiples of 10, they are placed in the main part of the right circle.
4 **210** 8 + 4 + 9 = 21 so 80 + 40 + 90 = 210
5 **£48.00** Refer to Test 5 Q10 and Test 10 Q4 on rounding; 7 is in the pounds place and another 7 is to its right, so 7 (in the pounds place) increases by 1 and the digits that follow change to 0.
6 **14 children** Use short division to find the answer; 7 goes into 9 once so write 1 above the 9; as there is a remainder of 2, carry this over to the next column to create the number 28; 7 goes into 28 four times, so write 4 above it.

$$\begin{array}{r} 14 \\ 7\overline{)9{}^28} \end{array}$$

7 **15 cm²** Count the squares to find the area.
8 **C** A right angle is 90°.
9 $\frac{3}{4}$ There are 16 squares altogether, so this is the denominator (bottom number); 12 are shaded so this is the numerator (top number). Simplify the fraction by dividing both numerator and denominator by the same number: 12 and 16 can both be divided by 4 (12 ÷ 4 = 3; 16 ÷ 4 = 4), so $\frac{12}{16} = \frac{3}{4}$
10 **cylinder**

Test 16: Mixed (page 22)

1–2

1:40 p.m. Refer to Test 3 Q7 on telling the time. The minute hand has just moved past 5 (5 mins × 5 = 25 mins) and points to 2 minutes after (25 + 2 = 27). The hour hand is shown halfway between 12 and 1 as the hour moves towards 1 pm. Refer to Test 14 Q2 on calculating elapsed time: 12:27 + 1 hr = 1:27 and 13:27 + 13 mins = 1:40

3 **C** Refer to Test 5 Q10 on rounding; 0 is in the tens place and 3 is to its right, so 0 remains the same and the following digits change to 0.

4 **40, 14** Refer to Test 2 Q7 on sequences; 13 has been subtracted each time: 53 − 13 = 40; 40 − 13 = 27; 27 − 13 = 14

5 **B** 1 whole turn = 360°; 90 + 270 = 360

6–7 **Kyle, girls** 20 + 30 + 27 = 77 picked by the girls; 44 + 12 + 8 = 64 picked by the boys.

8 **21** Refer to Test 8 Q3 on partitioning; 42 = 40 + 2; 40 ÷ 2 = 20 and 2 ÷ 2 = 1; 20 + 1 = 21

9 **550 ml** Refer to Test 9 Q6 on column subtraction; 1000 − 450 = 550

10 **0.8** Refer to Test 2 Q9 and use the place value grid to help write the answer; 10 has 1 zero so move the number 1 place to the right; 8 ÷ 10 = 0.8

Test 17: Mixed (page 23)

1 **8799, 7909, 7889, 7809** Refer to Test 2 Q3 and use the place value grid to help. Write the numbers in the grid and look for the largest number in the first column; if any numbers are the same, find the largest number in the next column.

2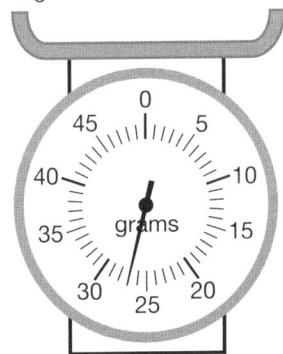

Between each 5 g, the scale has been separated into 5 equal parts. Therefore each small line represents 1 g (5 g ÷ 5 = 1 g) so an arrow points to the second small line after 25 (25 + 2 = 27).

3

Refer to Test 1 Q2 on different types of lines.

4 **D** Refer to Test 2 Q4 on negative numbers.

5 **£2.45** £1.00 = 100p so change the amounts to pence to make the calculations easier and refer to Test 9 Q6 on column subtraction; 150p + 60p + 45p = 255p; 500 − 255 = 245; 245p = £2.45

6 **17** Write as a missing number sentence (33 + □ = 50) and complete the inverse by subtracting: 50 − 33 = 17

7 **Rule = +15** Refer to Test 2 Q7 on sequences; 10 + 15 = 25

8 **25 cm** 1 m = 100 cm; Refer to Test 15 Q6 on short division and divide by 4 to find $\frac{1}{4}$; 100 ÷ 4 = 25

9 **15 mice** 3 × 5 = 15

10 **parallelogram** A parallelogram is a four-sided shape with opposite sides that are parallel.

Test 18: Mixed (pages 24–25)

1–2 **12, 2** 1 star = 4 children, so $\frac{1}{2}$ star = 2 children; 3 × 4 = 12 children; Class 4 has a half star more than Class 5 = 2 children.

3 **74 m** Refer to Test 1 Q10 on perimeter; 22 + 22 + 15 + 15 = 74

4 **A** Refer to Test 3 Q6 on regular and irregular polygons.

5–6 **8 cars. There will be 7 full cars and one car with only 2 children in it because 30 ÷ 4 = 7 r 2**

7 **approx. 37 kg** Between each 20 kg, the scale has been separated into 20 equal parts (20 kg ÷ 20 = 1 kg) therefore each small line represents 1 kg. The arrow points to the third small line before 40 kg and 40 − 3 = 37

8 **4** Refer to Test 3 Q3 on symmetry.

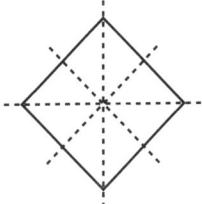

9 **250 kg** Refer to Test 2 Q9 and use the place value grid to help; as 10 has 1 zero, move the number 1 place to the left; 25 × 10 = 250

10 **518** Refer to Test 9 Q6 on column subtraction; 561 − 43 = 518

Test 19: Mixed (page 26)

1 **372** Refer to Test 11 Q8–9 on column addition and add in the same way as the decimal numbers shown.

2 **1 km**

3 **20** The number has been partitioned: 5721 = 5000 + 700 + <u>20</u> + 1

4 $4\frac{1}{4}, 4\frac{1}{2}, 5, 5\frac{1}{2}, 5\frac{3}{4}$ Use a number line, as shown, to help find the answer.

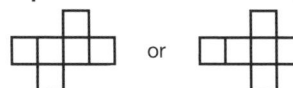

5 e.g. 45° is a half of a right angle.

6 e.g. An isosceles triangle has 2 sides that are the same length.

7 **C** Refer to Test 8 Q8 on multiples; $3 \times 3 = 9$; $3 \times 5 = 15$; $3 \times 8 = 24$

8 **Child's own number story for 120 − 56 = 64, e.g.** *On Wednesday there were 120 pupils who ate lunch at school. Of the 120 pupils 56 had school dinners meaning 64 had packed lunch.*

9–10 **3 adult tickets, £62.50** 2 children × 3 = 6 children, so 3 tickets need to be bought. Partition the amount into pounds and pence (£12.50 = £12.00 + 50p) then multiply the numbers by 5 (£12 × 5 = £60.00 and 50p × 5 = £2.50). Finally, add the answers together: £60.00 + £2.50 = £62.50

Test 20: Mixed (page 27)

1 **2350** The arrow is pointing to halfway between 2300 and 2400, so add the numbers together (2300 + 2400 = 4700) then divide by 2 (4700 ÷ 2 = 2350); refer to Test 15 Q6 on short division.

2 **2339** To find the smallest number, place the digits in order from smallest to largest.

3 **Two thousand, three hundred and thirty-nine** Refer to Test 2 Q3; writing the number in the place value grid may help find the answer.

4 **−4, 0** Refer to Test 2 Q4 on negative numbers and Test 2 Q7 on sequences.

5 $\frac{3}{10}$ 30 g of 100 g = $\frac{30}{100}$; refer to Test 15 Q9 on simplifying fractions; 30 and 100 can both be divided by 10 so $\frac{30}{100} = \frac{3}{10}$

6–7
Pets of children in Mrs Goddard's class		
Pet	Tally	Total
Dog	|||| ||||	9
Cat	|||| ||||		11
Hamster	||||	5
Pony			1

cat

8 **+** Because the answer is larger than the numbers, the equation will be addition or multiplication; 22 + 19 = 41; 22 × 19 = 418

9–10 **35 minutes, 12:55 p.m.** Refer to Test 11 Q1 to work backwards: 11:30 to 12:00 = 30 mins; 12:00 to 12:05 = 5 mins; 30 + 5 = 35 mins; Refer to Test 14 Q2 on calculating elapsed time: 12:05 + 30 mins = 12:35

Test 21: Mixed (pages 28–29)

1 **a rectangle drawn by child either 4 cm × 5 cm, 8 cm × 1 cm, 7 cm × 2 cm or 6 cm × 3 cm** Refer to Test 1 Q10 on perimeter. Half of 18 = 9 so 2 sides of the rectangle will add up to 9 cm. For example, 4 + 5 = 9 and 4 + 4 + 5 + 5 = 18

2 **a square either side of the row of four squares must be added e.g.**

3–4 **(5, 1)** Point C should be marked 8 squares along and 4 squares up, as shown. Refer to Test 3 Q6 on regular and irregular polygons; the points need to be the same distance apart (A and C are 6 squares apart so B and D will be the same); D is 5 squares along and 1 up (5, 1). The lines form a square when joined together.

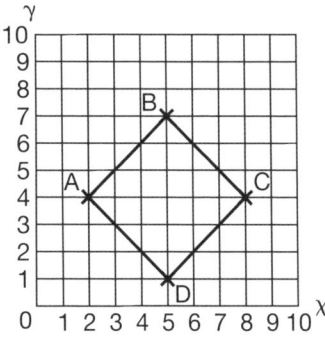

5 **967p** £1.00 = 100p so multiply by 100; refer to Test 2 Q9 on multiplying by 100; 9.67 × 100 = 967

6 **250** The equation is □ ÷ 10 = 25; use knowledge of times table or invert the equation to division (10 × 25 = 250)

7–8 **Jay and Lisa, No** Refer to Test 4 Q8–10 on reading bar charts; Jay and Lisa both swam 18 lengths; Liam swam fewer lengths than Beshar.

9 **156 miles** Refer to Test 9 Q6 on column subtraction; 253 − 97 = 156

10 **C**

Test 22: Mixed (page 30)

1 ◇ = **any number 271 to 277, inclusive, e.g. 274** '<' means less than so the number needs to be less than 278, but not less than 270.

2 **£12.27** Refer to Test 11 Q8–9 on column addition.

3 **27** Refer to Test 5 Q10 and Test 10 Q4 on rounding; 6 is in the place being rounded to and 9 is to its right, so 6 increases by 1.

4 **B** Refer to Test 2 Q4 on negative numbers.
5 **West** Refer to Test 1 Q9 on compass points.
6 **A** Refer to Test 8 Q8 on multiples; 6 × 9 = 54
7 **metres** Length is measured in mm, cm, m and km; metres are the most appropriate unit.
8 **6609** Add 1 to the 5 in the thousands place to find 6609.
9–10 **63, 9 boxes** 35 + 28 = 63; 63 ÷ 7 = 9

Test 23: Mixed (page 31)

1 **23.5, 23.36, 23.2, 23.19** Refer to Test 8 Q2 on ordering decimals.
2 **6** A right angle is 90°

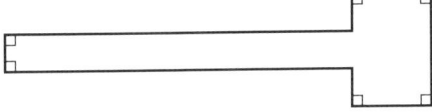

3 **A** Only 49 is in the 7 times table and can therefore be divided exactly by 7.
4 **30 cm** Refer to Test 1 Q10 on perimeter. A hexagon has 6 sides; 6 × 5 cm = 30 cm
5 **D** As 3 consecutive numbers need to be found, divide 30 by 3 (30 ÷ 3 = 10); then subtract 1 from the answer to find 9 and add 1 to find 11; 9 + 10 + 11 = 30
6 **△** The pattern is of a triangle followed by 2 chevrons.
7 **31**
8 **250 ml** Use repeated addition to find 3 lots of 250 (250 + 250 + 250 = 750); 1 litre = 1000 ml so subtract the answer from 1000 (1000 − 750 = 250); refer to Test 9 Q6 on column subtraction.
9 **30** To find a fraction of a number, divide the number by the denominator (bottom number) then multiply the answer by the numerator (top number); 40 ÷ 4 = 10 and 10 × 3 = 30
10 **168** Refer to Test 2 Q1 on column multiplication; 28 × 6 = 168

Test 24: Mixed (pages 32–33)

1 **B** A polygon is a closed shape with 3 or more sides.
2–3 **robins and wrens, 6** Refer to Test 4 Q8–10 on reading bar charts. Wrens and robins were both sighted 12 times, blue tits 6 times; 12 − 6 = 6
4 **+, ×** Add, subtract, multiply and divide 23 and 7 then repeat with 3 and 10 until an answer is found that is the same; 23 **+** 7 = 30 and 3 **×** 10 = 30
5 **133** Refer to Test 2 Q1 on column multiplication; 19 × 7 = 133
6 **3 hours 15 minutes** Refer to Test 14 Q2 on calculating elapsed time; 11:30 to 12:00 = 30 mins; 12:00 to 1:00 = 60 mins; 1:00 to 2:00 = 60 mins; 2:00 to 2:45 = 45 mins; 30 + 60 + 60 + 45 = 195 mins. There are 60 mins in 1 hr so 180 mins = 3 hrs; 195 − 180 = 15 mins
7 **e.g. C, E, T, U, W** Refer to Test 3 Q3 on symmetry.
8 **e.g.**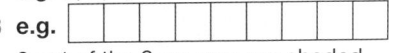
6 out of the 9 squares are shaded.
9 **A** The shape has 4 faces which are all triangular.
10 **1363** Refer to Test 11 Q8–9 on column addition; 476 + 887 = 1363

Test 25: Mixed (page 34)

1 **−6°C** Refer to Test 2 Q4 on negative numbers.
2 **332** Refer to Test 9 Q6 on column subtraction; 661 − 329 = 332
3 **4555** Subtract 1 from the 5 in the thousands place to find 4555
4 **None** Both have 6 faces.
5 **B** Refer to Test 1 Q10 on perimeter; 10 + 10 + 2 + 2 = 24; to find the area, multiply the lengths of 2 sides: 2 × 10 = 20
6 **(3, 5)** Point A is 3 squares along and 5 squares up. Always write how many squares along it is first.
7–8 **140 walks, 3 weeks** Refer to Test 2 Q9 and use the place value grid to multiply by 10: move the number 1 place to the left (14 × 10 = 140); use repeated addition to find how many lots of 14 go into 42 (14 + 14 + 14 = 42) so 3 lots of 14 = 3 weeks.
9 **74** Refer to Test 15 Q6 on short division; 148 ÷ 2 = 74
10 **A** 1 mile is approximately 1.6 km, therefore 1 mile is longer.

Test 26: Mixed (page 35)

1 **3** Invert the sum from division to multiplication and use knowledge of times tables to help (6 × 10 = 60); subtract 60 from 63 to find a remainder of 3.
2 **D** Refer to Test 15 Q9 on simplifying fractions; 6 and 8 can both be divided by 2 so $\frac{6}{8} = \frac{3}{4}$
3 **6 chicks** 1 in 2 is the same as $\frac{1}{2}$; $\frac{1}{2}$ of 12 = 6
4 **148 cm** 1.00 m = 100 cm; refer to Test 2 Q9 on multiplying by 100; 1.48 × 100 = 148
5 **49** 123 − 74 = 49
6 **0.75** Knowledge of basic decimal equivalents is needed here; $\frac{3}{4}$ = 0.75
7 **any three numbers divisible by 25 e.g. 50, 75, 100, etc.** Refer to Test 8 Q8 on multiples.
8 **e.g.** *water, milk, orange juice.* Millilitres are used to measure liquid.
9 **cylinder** A cylinder has 2 flat, circular faces and one curved face that connects them.

10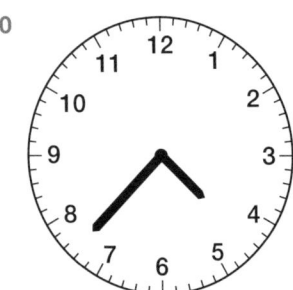

Refer to Test 3 Q7 on telling the time. The minute hand has just moved past 7 (5 mins × 7 = 35 mins) and points to 2 minutes after (35 + 2 = 37). The hour hand is shown halfway between 4 and 5 as the hour moves towards 5 p.m.

Test 27: Mixed (page 36)

1 **1.35** The line has been separated into ten equal parts so insert the decimal numbers as shown. Between each decimal number the line has been separated into another 10 equal parts and the arrow is pointing to the fifth small line after 1.3 therefore it is 1.35.

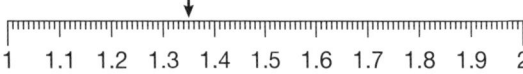

2 **45°** A right angle = 90°; 90 ÷ 2 = 45
3 **8999, 9889, 9898, 9988** Refer to Test 2 Q3 on ordering numbers.
4 **550** Invert the sum to 1000 − 450 and refer to Test 9 Q6 on column subtraction.
5 **D** Refer to Test 2 Q2 on adding fractions; $1 = \frac{10}{10}$ and $\frac{2}{10} + \frac{8}{10} = \frac{10}{10}$
6–7 **13, 90** Refer to Test 15 Q6 on short division. There are 4 children altogether including George (52 ÷ 4 = 13); 2 + 4 = 6 friends; refer to Test 2 Q1 on column multiplication (6 × 15 = 90)
8 **LIV** 50 = L; 4 = IV
9 **9025** Refer to Test 11 Q8–9 on column addition.
10 **28** Write the equation as a missing number sentence: □ − 3 ÷ 5 = 5. Work backwards through the equation, completing the inverse: 5 × 5 = 25 and 25 + 3 = 28

Test 28: Mixed (page 37)

1 **£1.21** Refer to Test 11 Q8–9 on column addition (£5.80 + £12.99 = £18.79). £1.00 = 100p so change the amounts to pence to make the subtraction easier (£20.00 = 2000p and £18.79 = 1879p) and refer to Test 9 Q6 on column subtraction; 2000 − 1879 = 121; 121p = £1.21
2–3 **45 minutes, 2:20 p.m.** Refer to Test 9 Q2 on calculating elapsed time; 11:20 to 12:00 = 40 mins and 12:00 to 12:05 = 5 mins; 40 + 5 = 45 mins. The only time shown after 1:42 p.m. is 2:20 p.m.
4 **5015** Refer to Test 2 Q3 and write the number in the place value grid to help find the answer.
5 **C** Look at a ruler to help guess the length.
6 **e.g.**

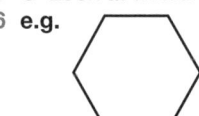

A hexagon is any closed shape with 6 sides.
7 **84** The function machine multiplies a number by 7 then adds 21; 9 × 7 = 63; 63 + 21 = 84
8 **Triangle should be in the middle section of the Venn diagram** Refer to Test 24 Q1 on polygons. A triangle is a polygon and has 3 corners therefore it is placed where the circles overlap.
9 **0.57** Refer to Test 2 Q9 and use the place value grid to help write the answer; as 100 has 2 zeros, move the number 2 places to the right; 57 ÷ 100 = 0.57
10 **1869** Refer to Test 2 Q1 on column multiplication; 267 × 7 = 1869

Puzzle 1 (page 38)

The child has to find as many different ways as possible (in 5 minutes) to make £6.75 using coins.

Puzzle 2 (page 39)

Refer to Test 2 Q7 on sequences. The difference between the numbers will show which times table each group can be found in.

2 times table 16 – 14 = 2; 18 – 16 = 2; 20 – 18 = 2
9 times table 45 – 36 = 9; 54 – 45 = 9; 63 – 54 = 9
5 times table 35 – 30 = 5; 40 – 35 = 5; 45 – 40 = 5
4 times table 20 – 16 = 4; 24 – 20 = 4; 28 – 24 = 4
8 times table 24 – 16 = 8; 32 – 24 = 8; 40 – 32 = 8
3 times table 24 – 21 = 3; 27 – 24 = 3; 30 – 27 = 3
7 times table 28 – 21 = 7; 35 – 28 = 7; 42 – 35 = 7
10 times table 60 – 50 = 10; 70 – 60 = 10; 80 – 70 = 10
6 times table 30 – 24 = 6; 36 – 30 = 6; 42 – 36 = 6

Puzzle 3 (page 40)

Cat characteristics	Tally	Total
black cat	|||	3
white cat	||	2
grey cat	||	2
big ears	|||	3
small ears	||||	4
long whiskers	|||||	5
short whiskers			1
no whiskers			1

There are **2** white cats.
More cats have **small ears**. (3 big, 4 small)
2 cats don't have long whiskers.

Puzzle 4 (page 41)

$\frac{1}{2}$ **of 48 = 24** $48 \div 2 = 24$

$\frac{3}{4}$ **is equivalent to** $\frac{9}{12}$ Refer to Test 15 Q9 on simplifying fractions; 9 and 12 can both be divided by 3 so $\frac{9}{12} = \frac{3}{4}$

What fraction is shaded? $\frac{3}{7}$ There are 7 sections altogether, so this is the denominator (bottom number); 3 are shaded so this is the numerator (top number).

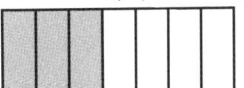

$\frac{3}{10} + \frac{7}{10} = 1$ Refer to Test 2 Q2 on adding fractions; $\frac{3}{10} + \frac{7}{10} = \frac{10}{10}$; $\frac{10}{10} = 1$

$\frac{1}{3}$ **of 15 = 5** $15 \div 3 = 5$

$\frac{2}{6} =$

There are 6 sections altogether, so this is the denominator (bottom number); 2 are shaded so this is the numerator (top number).

Which is the larger fraction, $\frac{2}{3}$ or $\frac{5}{6}$? $\frac{5}{6}$ Draw the fractions in a table, as shown, to compare their size.

$\frac{1}{3}$		$\frac{1}{3}$		$\frac{1}{3}$	
$\frac{1}{6}$	$\frac{1}{6}$	$\frac{1}{6}$	$\frac{1}{6}$	$\frac{1}{6}$	$\frac{1}{6}$

What fraction is shaded? $\frac{4}{9}$ There are 9 sections altogether, so this is the denominator (bottom number); 4 are shaded so this is the numerator (top number).

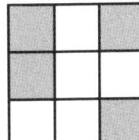

$\frac{2}{3}$ **is equivalent to** $\frac{4}{6}$ Refer to Test 15 Q9 on simplifying fractions; 4 and 6 can both be divided by 2 so $\frac{4}{6} = \frac{2}{3}$.

Puzzle 5 (page 42)

2D shapes are 'flat' and have sides and/or corners; 3D shapes have faces, vertices (corners) and edges and can be held.

one flat face and one curved face that narrows to a point = cone
Refer to Test 1 Q8
three sides, two the same length and one a different length = isosceles triangle
Refer to Test 19 Q6
the shape of a cereal box = cuboid
Refer to Test 6 Q6
two flat faces, one curved face = cylinder
Refer to Test 26 Q9
the shape of a ball = sphere
six flat faces, all edges the same length = cube
four triangular faces = tetrahedron (triangular-based pyramid)
Refer to Test 24 Q9
2D closed shape with straight lines = polygon
Refer to Test 24 Q1 on polygons.

NOTES

Test 17: Mixed

Test time: 0 — 5 — 10 minutes

1 Rewrite these numbers in order, largest first.

7809   7909   7889   8799

_____ _____ _____ _____

2 Show 27 g on this set of scales.

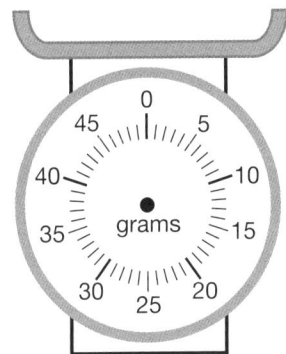

3 Draw a vertical line.

4 Circle the lowest temperature.

A −5°C   B 15°C   C 5°C   D −15°C

5 Harry took £5.00 to spend on a school trip.

He spent £1.50 on some sweets, 60p on a pencil and 45p on a drink.

How much money did Harry take home? _____

6 Two numbers have the sum of 50. One number is 33.

What is the other number?

_____

7 Write the rule explaining this sequence.

10   25   40   55   70   85

_____

_____

8 How many cm equal $\frac{1}{4}$ of a metre?

_____ cm

9 Every day Tilly the cat catches 3 mice. How many mice would she catch in 5 days?

_____

10 Name this shape.

_____

Total

TEST 18: **Mixed**

Test time: 0 5 10 minutes

1-2

Look carefully at the pictogram.

How many children in Class 3 receive more than £1.00 a week?

_____

How many more children in Class 4 than Class 5 receive more than £1.00 a week?

_____

Children who receive more than £1.00 pocket money a week

Class 1	☆ ☆
Class 2	☆
Class 3	☆ ☆ ☆
Class 4	☆ ☆ ☆ ☆ ☆
Class 5	☆ ☆ ☆ ☆

☆ = 4 children

3

Find the perimeter of Gary's house.

_____ m

22 m
Gary's house
15 m

4

Which of the following shapes are regular polygons?

1 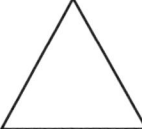   2 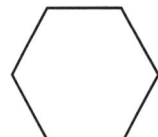   3    4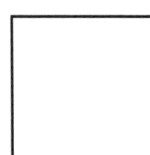

Circle the correct answer.

A 1, 2, 4   **B** 2, 3, 4   **C** 1, 4   **D** 3, 4

5-6

A school trip has been organised. Pupils are travelling in cars.
Each car can take 4 children.
How many cars will be needed for a class of 30 children? _____ cars

Explain your answer.

_____

_____

_____

7

These scales show the weight of Barney the dog.
Approximately how much does Barney weigh?

_____

8

How many lines of symmetry does this shape have?

____

9

A farmer's bag of chicken feed weighs 25 kg.

How much would 10 bags weigh?   _____ kg

10

Subtract 43 from 561.   _____

Test 19: Mixed

Test time: 0 — 5 — 10 minutes

1

Complete the number sentence.

345 + 27 = _____

2

1000 m = _____ km

3

5721 = 5000 + 700 + _____ + 1

4

Put these fractions in order, smallest first.

$5 \quad 4\frac{1}{2} \quad 5\frac{3}{4} \quad 4\frac{1}{4} \quad 5\frac{1}{2}$

____ ____ ____ ____ ____

5

Draw an angle smaller than 45°.

6

Draw an isosceles triangle.

7

Which of the following options shows three multiples of 3.
Circle the correct answer.

A 12, 16, 24 **B** 12, 19, 30

C 9, 15, 24 **D** 15, 21, 32

8

Write a number story that reflects the following;

120 − 56 = 64

_____

_____

_____

_____

9-10

Paws Wildlife Park was running a special offer.

With every adult ticket bought, two children could get in free.

How many adult tickets would need to be bought to get 6 children in free?

_____

Each adult ticket costs £12.50.
How much would 5 adult tickets cost?

£ _____

Total

Test 20: Mixed

Test time: 0 — 5 — 10 minutes

1. Look at this number line.

2300 — ↑ — 2400

Estimate the whole number the arrow is pointing at.

_____

2. Rearrange these digits to make the smallest whole number you can.

9 3 2 3   _____

3. Write, in words, the number you have just made in Question 2.

_____

_____

_____

4. Complete this sequence.

_____   −3   −2   −1   _____

5. What fraction is 30 g of 100 g?

_____

6-7. Complete the frequency table.

Pets of children in Mrs Goddard's class		
Pet	Tally	Total
Dog	|||| ||||	
Cat		11
Hamster		5
Pony			

Which is the most popular pet in Mrs Goddard's class?

_____

8. Add the missing sign.

22 ____ 19 = 41

9-10. Kate had to have an early lunch as she had a dentist appointment at 12:25 p.m.

Usually she ate her lunch at 12:05 p.m. but she was allowed to have lunch at 11:30 a.m. How many minutes earlier did she eat her lunch?

_____ mins

The dentist was running 30 minutes late. What time did Kate see the dentist?

_____

Total

Test 21: Mixed

Test time: 0 — 5 — 10 minutes

1

Draw a rectangle with a perimeter of 18 cm.

2

Finish the net of this shape.

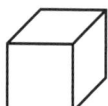
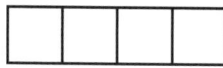

3-4

Point A is found at: 2 squares along and 4 squares up. This is written as (2,4).

Point B is at (5,7)

Mark point C on the grid at (8,4).

Mark point D on the grid to complete the regular polygon. Join the points.

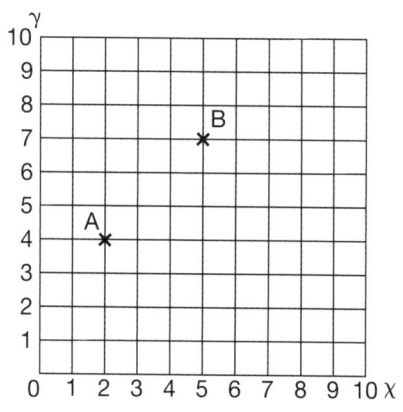

5

How many pence is £9.67? _____ p

6

I am thinking of a number. If you divide it by 10 then the answer is 25.

What number am I thinking of? _____

7-8

Look at the bar chart.

Who swam the most lengths?

_____

Did Beshar swim the least number of lengths?

_____

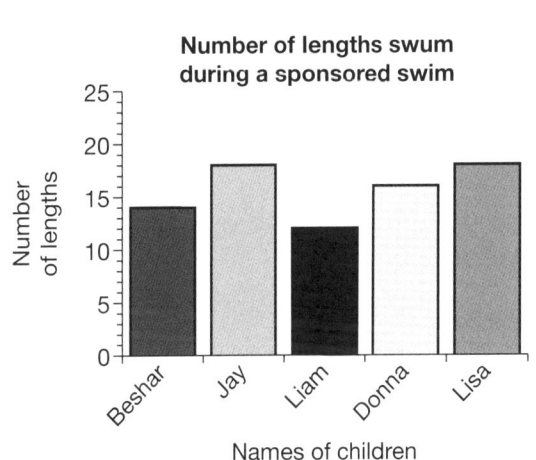

9

The Jenkins family are going on holiday to Wales. They have to go 253 miles to the campsite. They have a break at a motorway café after 97 miles.

How many more miles do they have to travel? _____ miles

10

Read the following statement, and then circle the correct answer.
It takes approximately _____ seconds to walk the width of a tennis court.

A 1 second   B 2 seconds   C 10 seconds   D 45 seconds

Total

TEST 22: **Mixed**

Test time: 0 — 5 — 10 minutes

1

What whole number could ◇ be?

$$270 < ◇ < 278$$

◇ = _____

2

£5.52
+£6.75

£ _____

3

Round 26.9 to the nearest whole number.

_____

4

Circle the temperature that is lower than −9°C.

A −8°C **B** −10°C **C** −7°C **D** −2°C

5

Gavin is facing North. While holding the compass, he turns 90° to the left. In which direction is he facing now?

_____

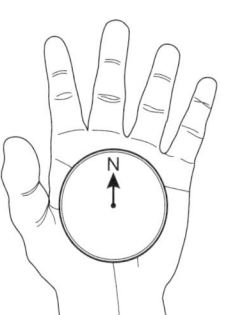

6

Which of these numbers is a multiple of 6 and 9?
Circle the answer.

A 54 **B** 15 **C** 69 **D** 32

7

Which unit of measure would you be most likely to use if you wanted to measure the distance from one side of the playground to the other?

_____

8

Find 1000 more than 5609.

_____

9-10

Daniel helped to pick lettuces on a farm in the holidays.

In one hour he picked 35 and in the second hour he picked 28.

How many lettuces did he pick in two hours?

_____

The lettuces then had to be packed in boxes. Each box held 7 lettuces.

How many boxes did Daniel need for the lettuces he picked?

_____

Test 23: Mixed

Test time: 0 – 10 minutes

1. List these decimals in order, largest first.

23.2   23.5   23.36   23.19

_____   _____   _____   _____

2. How many right angles can be found inside this shape?

_____

3. Which of these numbers is exactly divisible by 7?

A 49   B 29   C 69   D 39

4. Each side of a hexagon is 5 cm. What is the perimeter of the hexagon?

_____

5. Which three consecutive numbers add up to 30. Circle the answer.

A 8, 9, 10   B 10, 11, 12
C 7, 8, 9   D 9, 10, 11

6. Look carefully at this repeating sequence. What will be the next symbol?

△ > > △ > > △ > > ___

7. How many days are there in July?

_____

8. Three friends were thirsty. A litre of juice was made. Each child had 250 ml.

How much juice was left after the friends had drunk their drinks?

_____

9. What is $\frac{3}{4}$ of 40?

_____

10. Frome School had six classes. There were 28 children in each class.

How many children went to Frome School?

_____

TEST 24: **Mixed**

Test time: 0 — 5 — 10 minutes

1

Circle the polygon.

A  B C D

2-3

This bar chart shows the results of a bird survey.

Which two types of birds were sighted the same number of times?

_____ _____

How many more wrens were seen than blue tits?

_____

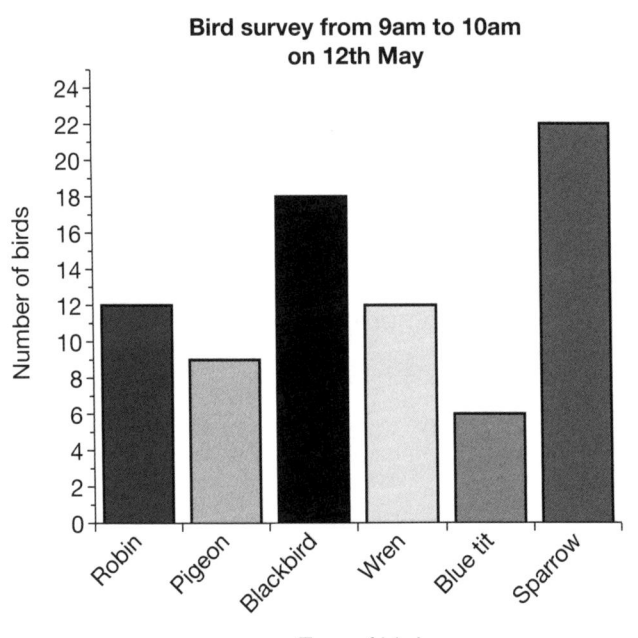

4

Add the missing signs to make this correct.

23 ____ 7 = 3 ____ 10

5

For seven weeks in a row Aimee got 19 out of 20 for her spelling test.

How many spellings did she get right over all seven weeks? _____

6

A train leaves London for Newcastle at 11:30 a.m. It arrives in Newcastle at 2:45 p.m. How long did the journey take?

_____ hrs _____ mins

7

Draw a capital letter from the alphabet that only has one line of symmetry.

8

Shade $\frac{6}{9}$ of this shape.

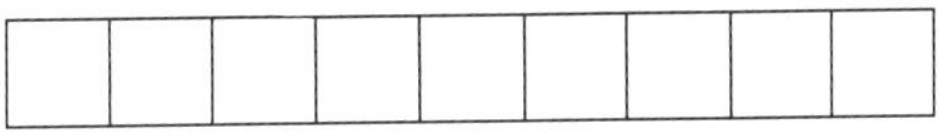

9

Look at this 3D shape. What is it?
Circle the correct answer.

A tetrahedron

B polyhedron

C pyramid

D sphere

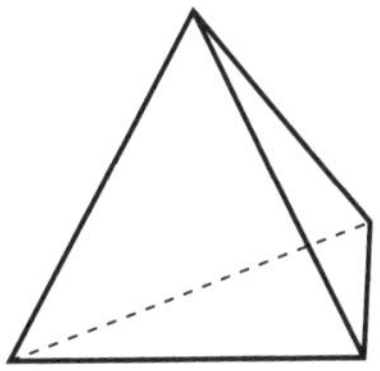

10

Total 476 and 887. _____

Total

Test 25: Mixed

Test time: 0 5 10 minutes

1
The temperature outside is −5°C. An hour later the temperature drops another degree. What is the temperature now?

_____ °C

2
Subtract 329 from 661.

_____

3
Find 1000 less than 5555.

_____

4
How many more faces does a cuboid have compared to a cube?

_____

5
Circle the correct perimeter (P) and area (A) of this shape.

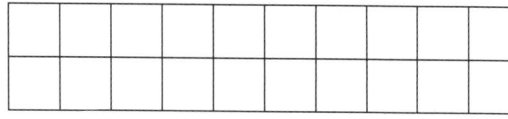

A P = 20 A = 20 **B** P = 24 A = 20
C P = 20 A = 24 **D** P = 24 A = 24

6
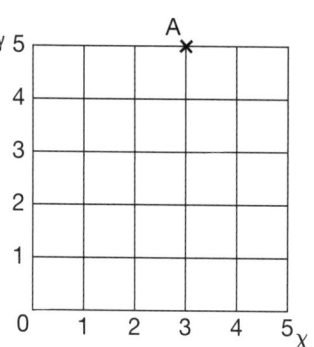

Point A is at (_____, _____) on the grid.

7-8
Holly the dog has 14 walks a week.

How many walks does she have during 10 weeks?

_____

Unfortunately Holly was ill and missed 42 walks.

How many weeks of walks did she miss?

_____

9
Halve 148.

_____

10
Circle the correct answer.

A mile is _____ a kilometre.

A more than   **B** less than

Test 26: Mixed

Test time: 0 — 5 — 10 minutes

1 If 63 is divided by 10 what is the remainder?

___

2 Circle an equivalent fraction of $\frac{3}{4}$.

A $\frac{3}{5}$ **B** $\frac{4}{8}$ **C** $\frac{6}{9}$ **D** $\frac{6}{8}$

3 A chicken sat on 12 eggs waiting for them to hatch.
Eventually 1 in every 2 eggs hatched. How many chicks hatched?

___

4 Convert 1.48m to centimetres.

_____ cm

5 Michelle collected unusual animal models. By the age of 8 she had collected 74. By the age of 9 she had collected 123.
How many models did she collect between the ages 8 to 9?

___

6 Write the decimal form of the fraction $\frac{3}{4}$. _____

7 Write three numbers that are multiples of 25.

_____ _____ _____

8 Write an item that you would use millilitres to measure.

_____

9 What shape is this a net of?

_____

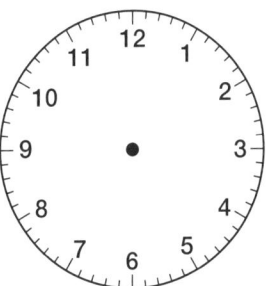

10 Steven leaves home to meet his friends at 4:37.
Mark this time on the clock face.

Test 27: Mixed

Test time: 0 — 5 — 10 minutes

1 What number is the arrow pointing to?

_____

2 How many degrees equal half a right angle?

_____ °

3 Order these whole numbers, smallest first.

9988   9898   8999   9889

_____ _____ _____ _____

4 Write in the missing number.

1000 − _____ = 450

5 Circle the correct answer.

$\frac{2}{10} + ? = 1$

A $\frac{1}{2}$ B $\frac{9}{10}$ C $\frac{2}{3}$ D $\frac{8}{10}$

6-7 After school on Monday George and his 3 friends ate 52 strawberries. If they all ate the same number how many strawberries did they each eat?

_____

On Tuesday two more friends joined the group. This time each child ate 15 strawberries. How many strawberries were eaten in total on Tuesday?

_____

8 Write the roman numeral for 54.

_____

9 3327 + 5698 = _____

10 Carys thinks of a number. She subtracts 3 then divides it by 5. The answer is 5.
What number did Carys start with?

_____

Test 28: Mixed

Test time: 0 – 10 minutes

1

Raiza spent £5.80 on a book and £12.99 on a DVD.

How much change did she have from £20.00?

_____

2-3

Tours of the castle were being given at the following times.

| 11:20 a.m. | 12:05 p.m. | 12:50 p.m. | 1:35 p.m. | 2:20 p.m. |

How many minutes were there between each tour?

_____

If you arrived for a tour at 1:42 p.m. what time would your tour leave?

_____

4

Write five thousand and fifteen as a number.

_____

5

Approximately how long is this line? Circle the correct answer.

A 0.5 cm **B** 2.5 cm **C** 5 cm **D** 10 cm

6

Draw a hexagon.

7

9 → ×7 → +21 → ____

8

Place this shape correctly into the Venn diagram. △

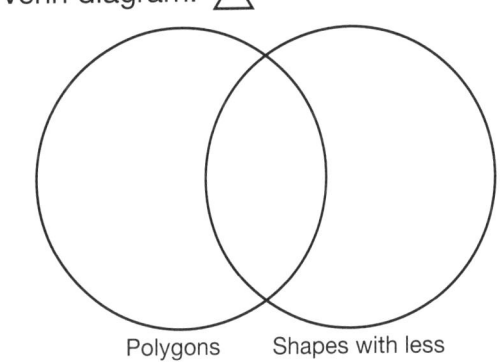

Polygons   Shapes with less than 4 corners

9

Divide 57 by 100.

_____

10

Multiply 267 by seven.

_____

Time for a break! Go to Puzzle Page 42

Total

Puzzle 1

Making money

In 5 minutes, how many different ways can you make this amount?

You can only use coins.

Remember the coins you can use are…

£6.75

You can use each coin as many times as you like.

Example: £2 + £2 + £1 + £1 + 50p + 20p + 5p

Puzzle 2

Times table hunt

Look carefully at these number sequences.

Each sequence is made up of multiplication facts.

Which times table can each sequence be found in?

- 14 16 18 20 ➡ _____ times table
- 36 45 54 63 ➡ _____ times table
- 30 35 40 45 ➡ _____ times table
- 16 20 24 28 ➡ _____ times table
- 16 24 32 40 ➡ _____ times table
- 21 24 27 30 ➡ _____ times table
- 21 28 35 42 ➡ _____ times table
- 50 60 70 80 ➡ _____ times table
- 24 30 36 42 ➡ _____ times table

Puzzle ③

Cat characteristics

Look carefully at the picture and complete the frequency table.

Cat characteristics	Tally	Total
black cat	|||	3
white cat		
grey cat		
big ears		
small ears		
long whiskers		
short whiskers		
no whiskers		

Answer these questions.

How many of the cats are white? _____

Do more cats have big or small ears? _____

How many cats do not have long whiskers? _____

Puzzle 4

Fraction match

Use a line to link the fraction with its answer.

$\frac{1}{2}$ of 48 =

$\frac{3}{4}$ is equivalent to

What fraction is shaded?

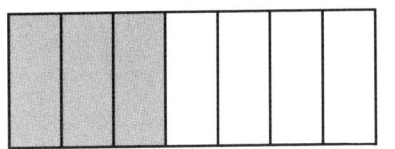

$\frac{3}{10} + \frac{7}{10} =$

$\frac{1}{3}$ of 15 =

Which is the larger fraction, $\frac{2}{3}$ or $\frac{5}{6}$?

$\frac{2}{6} =$

What fraction is shaded?

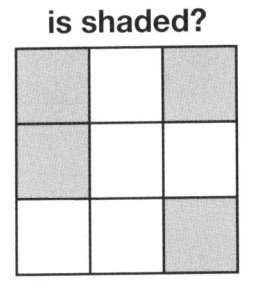

$\frac{2}{3}$ is equivalent to

$\frac{3}{7}$

$\frac{9}{12}$

24

1

5

$\frac{5}{6}$

$\frac{4}{9}$

$\frac{4}{6}$

Puzzle 5

Guess the shape

Read the clues carefully and write the shape they are describing.
Watch out, they can be 2D or 3D shapes!

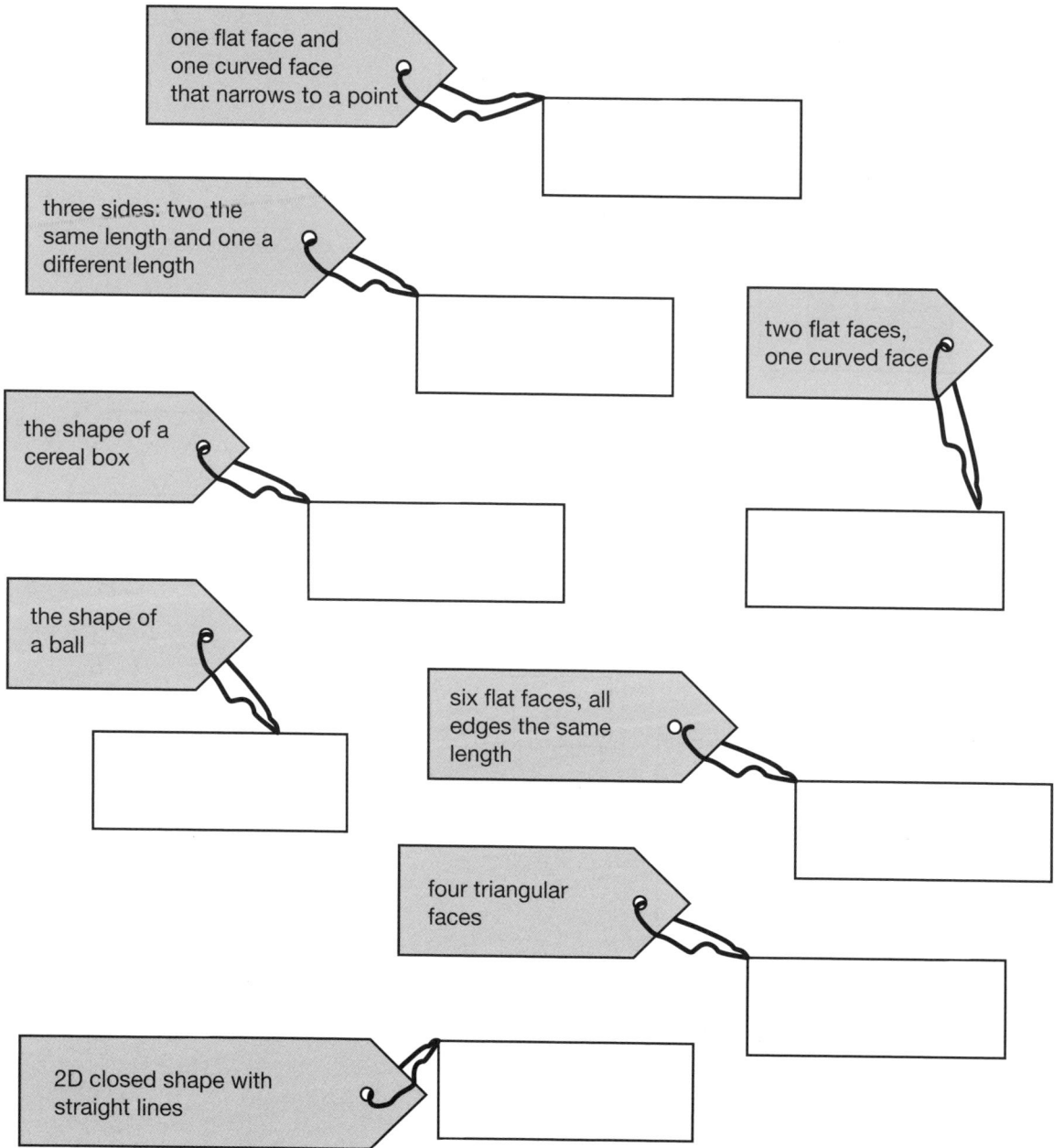

Progress Grid

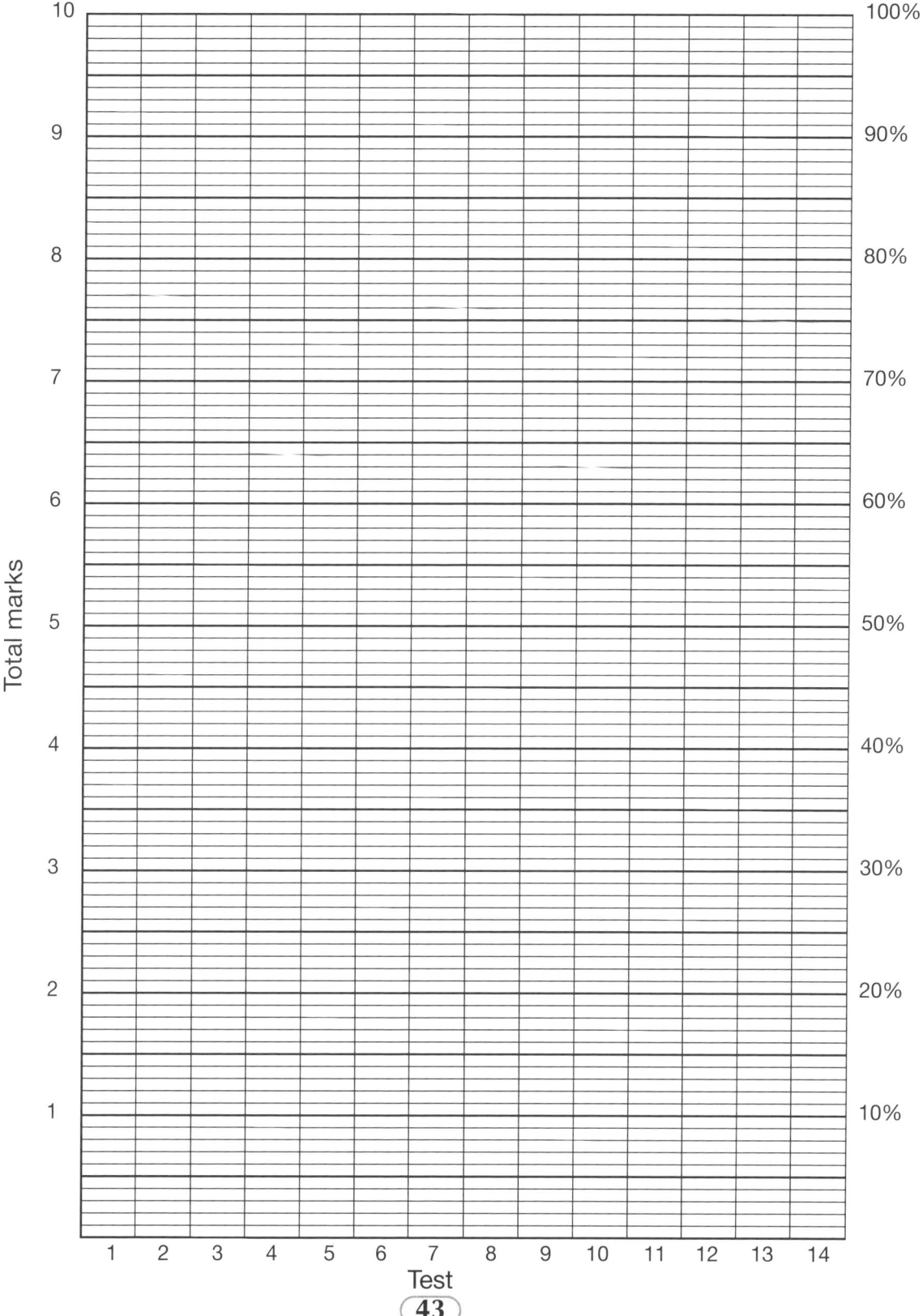

Progress Grid

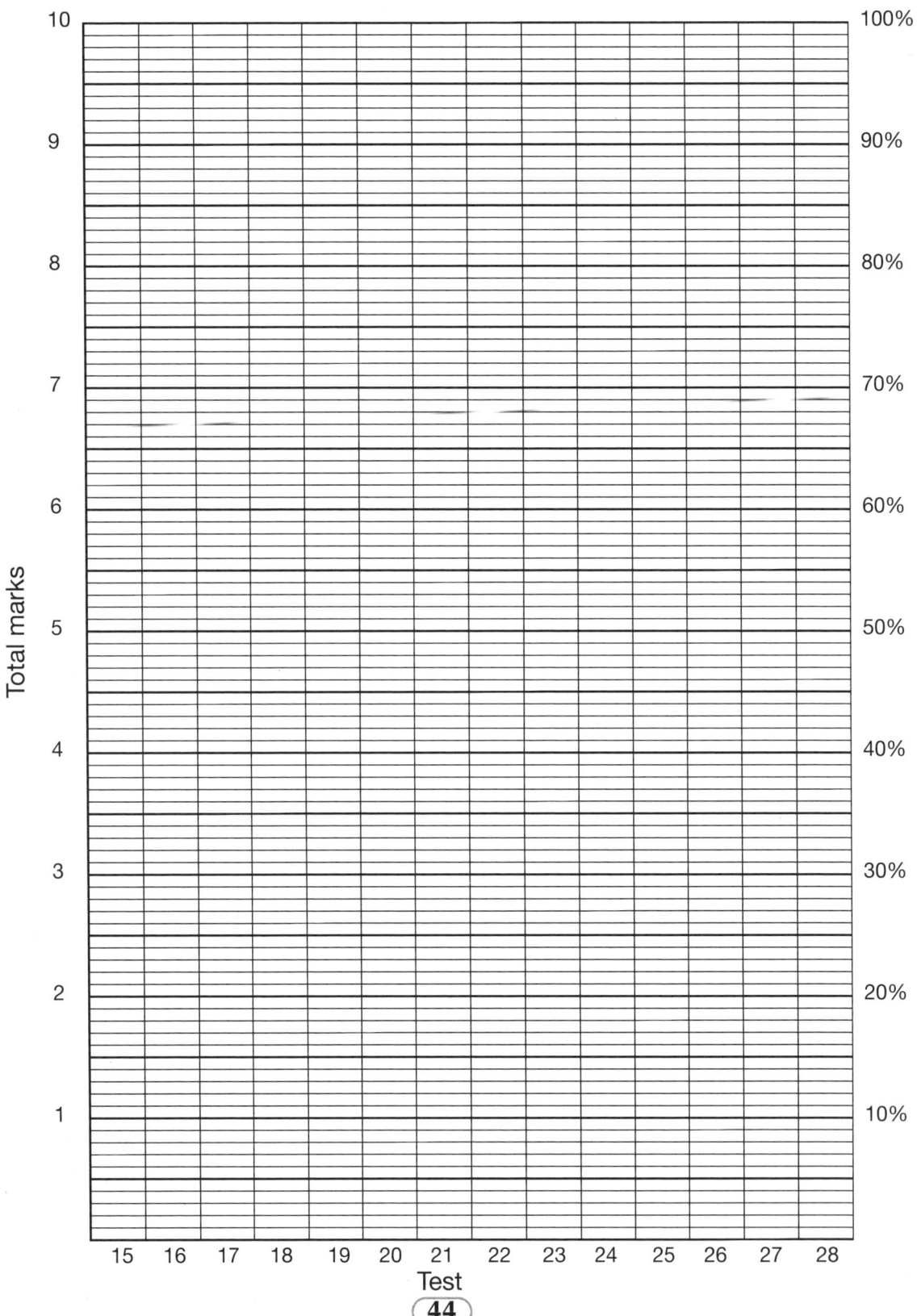

44